AMERICA'S UNELECTED GOVERNMENT

National Institute of Public Affairs

AMERICA'S UNELECTED GOVERNMENT: Appointing the President's Team

JOHN W. MACY
BRUCE ADAMS
J. JACKSON WALTER

Senior Consultant: G. Calvin Mackenzie

A National Academy of Public Administration Book

BALLINGER PUBLISHING COMPANY
Cambridge, Massachusetts
A Subsidiary of Harper & Row, Publishers, Inc.

The National Institute of Public Affairs
is the educational affiliate of the
National Academy of Public Administration

1120 G Street, N.W., Suite 540
Washington, D.C. 20005

Funding for this project was provided by
The Business Roundtable
and
The George Gund Foundation

International Standard Book Number: 0-88410-964-X (C)
0-88410-965-8 (P)

Library of Congress Catalog Card Number: 83-15540

Printed in the United States of America

Library of Congress Cataloging in Publication Data

Macy, John W., 1917-
America's unelected government.

At head of title: National Institute of Public Affairs.
Includes bibliographical references and index.
1. United States—Officials and employees—Appointment, qualifications, tenure, etc. 2. Government executives—United States—Appointment, qualifications, tenure, etc. 3. Presidents—United States—Staff. I. Adams, Bruce, 1947- II. Walter, J. Jackson, 1940- . III. Title.
JK736.M335 1983 353.03'2 83-15540
ISBN 0-88410-964-X
ISBN 0-88410-965-8 (pbk.)

CONTENTS

LIST OF FIGURES AND TABLES

Figures

Tables

PREFACE

The government of the United States is run not by career ministers but by amateurs. The Founding Fathers set up this system of citizen government in the spirit of Cincinnatus and it has thrived for 200 years. To be sure, there is the Civil Service—now celebrating its centennial—that provides continuity and expertise, and there is a supporting cast of full-time government and political watchers, campaign managers, party officials, lobbyists, pollsters, and public policy experts. But these folks generally don't get the cabinet and subcabinet posts that are the subject of this book. Those who do are the "in-and-outers," that is, the executives, lawyers, professors, and financiers who follow the election results back and forth between the public and private sectors.

This book is about how the in-and-outers come in, whether for a first or a repeat tour, and it suggests that we have gone to great lengths to make it difficult for our system to work and to govern well. The evidence is compelling:

- The unrelenting antigovernment rhetoric of our past two national campaigns boomerangs when many prospective presidential appointees decline job offers because of a reluctance to join up with such a discredited organization as the federal government.
- The media's coverage of a president's personnel recruiting efforts, particularly during the postelection transition crunch, achieves a

circuslike quality that trivializes the central political and strategic issues that are at stake.

- Too many private employers not only discourage their best managers from taking off for periods of government service but also design compensation and promotion systems that emphasize this policy of discouragement and reinforce the characterization of the federal government as a natural adversary of American business.
- Very little is done to teach new appointees the ropes, to work out with them the differences in standards of conduct appropriate for public as opposed to private officials or to school them in the best techniques for performing the jobs in which they will serve.
- Because not enough careful analysis and recording has been done of the in-and-outers process—of the presidential personnel recruiting and appointing system—a wasteful, even embarrassing, "reinvent-the-wheel" quality characterizes most postelection transitions.

Certainly it does not have to be this way. Based on the testimony of keen observers of this activity since the Truman and Eisenhower administrations, and supported by my own experience as the first director of the U.S. Office of Government Ethics, appointed by President Carter and reappointed by President Reagan, I am convinced that a deficient presidential personnel appointment process poses very real risks to our country. I know that the obvious defects in the current process can be cured, I believe that the recommendations in Chapter 6 of this book represent sensible first steps, and I recognize that this study can only be the beginning.

This book suggests several ways to improve management in the rough and tumble of power politics. There are too many interests, passions, and considerations involved in choosing a cabinet for it to be a genteel endeavor. It must be the president's responsibility just as much as the selection of a company's top executives has to be the job of—and a major source of power of—a corporate chief executive officer. But it is also the president's responsibility to appoint men and women whose competence, integrity, creativity, and political sensitivity will serve the nation well. When too many appointees fail their presidents, as they have recently, it becomes necessary carefully to assess and improve the underlying system.

This book does that. It sketches out the problems and recommends five sets of initiatives that are needed in order to shorten the odds that presidents will make consistently sound personnel decisions. These are to:

1. broaden the pool of willing, able, and competent people from which presidential appointees are selected (Recommendations 1–5);
2. manage the recruiting and appointing process by reaching out to those in the broadened pool (Recommendations 6–14);
3. clarify the rules, especially those concerning conflicts of interest and standards of conduct, that apply to federal officials (Recommendations 15–18);
4. ease the two-way transition between private and public sector employment, especially for younger and first-time presidential appointees (Recommendations 19–21); and
5. adopt the views of the experts by uncoupling the linkage between legislative and executive branch salaries (Recommendation 22).

These recommended initiatives may not seem charged with the feistiness and intensity of the presidential politics that swirl around them, but I know these issues are real ones and I am convinced these recommendations are realistic. If they are carried out in the spirit we offer them, the capacity of our nation to govern itself will be enhanced.

On behalf of the National Academy of Public Administration, I wish to express my thanks to The Business Roundtable for its support of this project.

Washington, D.C.
June 1983

J. Jackson Walter
President
National Academy of
Public Administration

ACKNOWLEDGMENTS

The research for this report was conducted in several ways. The authors drew heavily on their own backgrounds as participants in and students of the appointment process. They read broadly in the literature on government personnel and presidential appointments. They examined the statutes, regulations, reporting forms, and other documents that govern the formalities of the appointment process. Interviews were conducted with a wide variety of people who have had direct experience in that process, with some of the country's leading students of the presidency, and with individuals in the private sector who have been well positioned to reflect on the strengths and weaknesses of the appointment process. A list of those reviewers, commenters, and interviewees follows. We deeply appreciate their assistance with this project and, of course, we absolve them of any responsibility for its findings or recommendations. Those names preceded by an asterisk are members of the National Academy of Public Administration.

Decker Anstrom
*Robert Ball
*James M. Beggs
Douglas J. Bennet
*Robert P. Biller
Michael Blumenthal
Sam W. Brown, Jr.
James McGregor Burns
Michael Cardozo
John Clinton
*Murray Comarow
Joseph Coors

Donald Dawson
*Marshall Dimock
Scott Ellsworth
Dan H. Fenn, Jr.
*James Fesler
Fred Fielding
*Arthur Flemming
*A. Lee Fritschler
*John Gardner
*Bernard Gladieux
Fred I. Greenstein
Erwin Hargrove
Alexander Heard
*Bernard F. Hillenbrand
John H.F. Hoving
E. Pendleton James
*Haynes Johnson
William Stewart Johnson
*Roger W. Jones
Susan B. King
Winthrop Knowlton
Martin Krasney
*Carol C. Laise
W.R. Liebtag
Avery Lieserson
*Hugh McKinley
Fred Malek
*Larry Margolis
David Mathews
Samuel L. Maury
Arnie Miller
William Miller
*James M. Mitchell
*Frederick Mosher
*E.K. Nelson
*Richard Neustadt
David Newsom
*Frank Pace
*William Parsons
*Bradley H. Patterson, Jr.
Peter Peterson
Nelson Polsby
John Post
Austin Ranney
*Elliott Richardson
*Henry Reining
*Ray Remy
*Elmer Staats
*David T. Stanley
Robert S. Strauss
Warren G. Sullivan
Dennis F. Thompson
Alexander Trowbridge
Charles R. Warren
*W. Harrison Wellford
*Roger Wilcox
Walter Williams
*Alfred M. Zuck

Chapter 1

INTRODUCTION

For two weeks in October 1962, a group of people known as the Executive Committee of the National Security Council met around the clock in a furtive search for ways to head off a nuclear confrontation between the Soviet Union and the United States. Of its members, one was the president of the United States, several were former presidential appointees called back into consultation, and the rest were incumbent presidential appointees. The president was the only elected official in the group.

From 1965 through 1968 a small group of men gathered once a week at the White House to plot the conduct of the Vietnam War. Generally included in the group were the president, the secretaries of state and defense, the chairman of the Joint Chiefs of Staff, the director of the Central Intelligence Agency, and several members of the White House staff. Only the president was an elected official; all of the others were presidential appointees.

For three days in August 1971, fifteen people gathered at Camp David for a meeting that the chairman of the Council of Economic Advisers called "one of the most dramatic events in the history of economic policy."[1] It was here that Richard Nixon and his senior advisers decided to establish a program of wage and price controls, one of the rare occasions when this has occurred in peacetime. Of the people at those meetings, all but Richard Nixon himself were presidential appointees.

In the American political system, there are two routes to high office. One is the electoral process. Because elections are so much a part of the landscape of American politics, this is the most visible route. But of the five million people (civilian and military) who serve the federal government in Washington and around the world only 537 obtain their jobs by winning an election.

The rest—the vast majority—follow the second path to power: the appointment process. Many of them secure their appointments by passing an exam or otherwise competing effectively on the basis of merit criteria for a position in the career service. The most important and influential of those in this second group, however, have a presidential appointment as their ticket to office. They are part of a president's administration because he asked them to be.

One of the ironies of political analysis in America is that the electoral process, which produces but a small percentage of those who hold important offices in the federal government, has always been the subject of intense scrutiny, study, and reform. The appointment process, on the other hand, and especially the selection of the highest ranking presidential appointees, has been studied little. Scholars and journalists have told us a great deal more about congressional primaries in South Dakota or Vermont than they have about the selection of secretaries of defense. We have shelves of books and reams of newspaper articles on every minute in the day of our presidential candidates, but we have very little that provides a genuine understanding of how—and how well—they construct their administrations after they have secured election.

The irony in this imbalance of information on the electoral and appointment processes is that, in terms of its impact on the day-to-day operation of the federal government, the latter is as important as the former. Public policy is shaped as much by those who are appointed to government as by those who are elected. In some areas—defense, international relations, regulatory policy—those who are appointed often play a larger direct role than those who are elected. Wise electoral choices avail us little if they are followed by unwise appointment decisions. As James M. Landis once noted in a report he prepared for president-elect John F. Kennedy: "The prime key to the improvement of the administrative process is the selection of qualified personnel. Good men can make poor laws workable; poor men will wreak havoc with good laws."[2]

The point is fundamental: we cannot have good government in the United States without good people making and implementing the important decisions. It follows that because so many of these people are selected in the appointment process, we cannot have good government unless we have an appointment process that is able consistently to identify and recruit government leaders with expertise, integrity, creativity, and political sensitivity.

"Ours is a difficult and exhilarating form of government," notes former cabinet member John Gardner, "not for the faint of heart, not for the tidy-minded, and in these days of complexity not for the stupid. We need men and women who can bring to government the highest order of intellect, social motivations sturdy enough to pursue good purposes despite setbacks, and a resilience of spirit equal to the frustrations of public life."[3] Now, more than ever, it is imperative that we have an appointment process capable of attracting our most talented citizens into the public service.

In this study we will examine the presidential appointment process as it has operated historically and as it operates today. We will focus on its strengths and on its flaws. It is our hope that we can identify those elements of the process that should be retained and recommend improvements for those that should not. We share the views of those most familiar with the appointment process: that it is critically important to the effective administration of the federal government and that the need for penetrating and comprehensive analysis of it is long overdue.

CHARACTER OF THE APPOINTMENT POWER

The Legalities

The president's legal authority to make appointments derives from two sources: the Constitution and the variety of statutes enacted over time to create new federal offices. The constitutional grant is a straightforward statement in Article II:

> [The President] shall nominate, and by and with the advice and consent of the Senate, shall appoint Ambassadors, other public Ministers and Consuls, Judges of the Supreme Court, and all other officers of the United States, whose appointments are not herein otherwise provided for, and which shall be established by law; but the Congress may by law vest the appointment of such inferior officers, as they think proper, in the President alone, in the courts of law, or in the heads of departments.

Because the clarity of this language has left little doubt about its intent or about the extent of the president's appointment power, this description of presidential appointment authority is perhaps the least litigated part of Article II. The only significant judicial interpretations of this section occurred in 1931 and in 1976. In 1931, in *United States* v. *Smith*, the Supreme Court held that the Senate could not revoke its consent to a nomination once an appointee had been installed in office. In 1976, in *Buckley* v. *Valeo*, the Court found unconstitutional a provision of the 1974 federal campaign act amendments, which provided for the appointments of four of the six members of the Federal Election Commission by the president pro tempore of the Senate and the Speaker of the House. The Court held that because this commission was an administrative agency with significant authority to make and enforce rules, its members had to be appointed by the president as required under Article II of the Constitution.

For most of our history, the president's authority to make appointments to the major offices of the government has not been in dispute. There has, however, been some inconsistency on two subsidiary issues: the definition of what constitutes an "officer of the United States" and determinations of the kinds of offices for which presidential appointments must be subject to the advice and consent of the Senate.

Because decisions on each of these matters have been scattered throughout our history, their outcomes have tended to reflect not some consistent legal principle but rather, contemporary concerns and particularly the contemporary status of relations between the president and Congress. In examining the table of organization for the federal government, it is not uncommon to find a bureau the chief of which is appointed by the president juxtaposed to another bureau of similar size and responsibility where the chief is appointed by a department head. Nor is it uncommon to find a pair of similar offices, both filled by presidential appointment but only one of which requires confirmation by the Senate. The political context of the statutes that created these positions, rather than some administrative logic or symmetry, is the reason for this peculiar pattern of inconsistency. To understand why the president's appointment authority reaches deeper in one department than in another, or why confirmation is required for some positions but not for others, one can only look to the unique legislative history from which each office sprang.

Another critical element in determining the character of the president's appointment authority is the Senate's role in reacting to his nominations. From our records of their deliberations it is quite clear that the Founding Fathers intended the president to be the initiator in the appointment process and for the Senate to serve as a potent check on the president's exercise of the appointment power. Alexander Hamilton wrote, for instance: "It is not likely that the Senate's sanction would often be refused, where there were not special and strong reasons for the refusal."[4]

Looking back over almost 200 years of historical practice, we can certify the accuracy of Hamilton's prediction. Though the extent and vigor of Senate involvement in the appointment process have ebbed and flowed, the characteristic pattern has been for the Senate to acquiesce with alacrity in all but the most controversial presidential appointments. In general, it has withheld its consent only in those rare cases when serious questions have arisen about the competence, integrity, policy views, or freedom from bias of a particular candidate for appointment. In the sharing of the appointment power mandated by the Constitution, the Senate has been a significant, but often silent, partner.

This study will not focus in detail on the Senate confirmation process. It will touch upon that process only insofar as the paperwork requirements of Senate committees and the occasional unpleasantness of confirmation hearings impede the president's efforts to attract good people to serve in his administration.

The Numbers

The number of presidential appointments is large or small depending upon one's perspective. Compared to the number of appointments made by executives in most other Western democracies, the president of the United States has a broad appointment power. A change in party majorities in Britain, for instance, usually results in about 75 administrative appointments by the new prime minister. In France, a new president will make about 25 major appointments to his administration and a maximum of 150 if one counts the subministers.

In some American states, however, a newly elected governor will have to fill far more offices than an American president. Even in some large cities, the number of appointments controlled by the mayor greatly exceeds the number made by a president.

The scope of the president's appointment power falls between these two extremes. In technical terms the president is responsible for making more than 75,000 appointments each year; however, the largest percentage of those are routine commissions and promotions in the armed forces, the Coast Guard, the National Oceanic and Atmospheric Administration, the Public Health Service, and the Foreign Service—hardly matters of great importance to a busy chief executive. In practice, the attention of the president and his personnel staff tends to focus primarily on the appointments for which he is the legal appointing authority. These are listed in Table 1-1.

The Appointment Cycle

The character of the president's appointment responsibilities is complicated further by the timing of appointment decisions—a matter over which he has little control. It is a painful irony for most administrations that the largest clusters of appointment opportunities come at the very beginning—a time when the president is least prepared or staffed to make them—and again late in the term, when recruiting is most difficult.

Appointments during the transition period are the most troublesome, for this is a time when a number of conflicting pressures are bearing down upon the president. His first appointments are matters of great symbolic importance because they are the first real acts of his administration, and journalists and politicians across the country will scrutinize them for hints about the character and policy direction of the administration. Contributors to the president's election victory will look to these early appointments for the rewards they

Table 1-1. Appointments for Which the President is Legal Appointing Authority (*as of June 1983*).

Type	*Number*
PAS[a] positions in cabinet departments	276
PAS positions in independent agencies and regulatory commissions	286
Full-time ambassadors	150
Judges, U.S. marshals, U.S. attorneys	950
Part-time PA[b] and PAS	2,263
Total	3,925

a. PAS = presidential appointment requiring Senate confirmation.
b. PA = presidential appointment not requiring Senate confirmation.
Source: Presidential Personnel Office and Executive Clerk of the White House.

think are the just desserts for their efforts in his behalf. Members of the president's party in Congress, knowing his desire to establish a good relationship with them, will urge him to find jobs in his administration for their staff members and constituents.

Meanwhile, the president will want these initial appointments to serve his own important purposes. He will want to select people whose loyalty and judgment he can trust. He will want to build teams that can work together when they share jurisdiction over critical issues like the economy or national security. He will want to pick appointees who can command the respect of the career civil servants and of foreign governments. And, of course, he will want people whose ability to do their jobs effectively is beyond doubt.

As if these pressures were not great enough, there is one more. To comb the country, to find people who fit these multiple requirements, to entice them to join his administration, and to prepare them for their new responsibilities, he has about seventy-five days. Given this set of circumstances, it is not surprising that the staffing of new presidential administrations has typically provided some of the least expert demonstrations of the art of American statecraft. One student of the appointment process in the transition period has described it as follows:

> The personnel choices a president makes during the transition period are perhaps as important collectively as any other set of decisions he will make during his time in office. Yet these choices are often made with inadequate preparation and often in a state of near ignorance of the kinds of jobs being filled and the real abilities of the people selected to fill them. So many matters of consequence press upon a president-elect during the transition that he never has adequate time to give to the direct examination of candidates and their qualifications, or even to the establishment of a set of procedures to permit his staff to carry out that function effectively in his stead. The typical result is a helter-skelter process with personnel choices made by a variety of individuals, each interpreting the President's priorities in his own way, each coping with a different set of political realities.[5]

If there is a beneficial outcome of this disorder it is that new presidents are forced quickly to recognize the arduousness of the appointment process and the need to manage it more effectively. With the single exception of Lyndon Johnson, no president since World War II has gone into the second year of his administration with the same procedures for selecting appointees that he employed at the outset.

For most presidents the transition and the early months of the first term have been a learning experience—in personnel matters often a painful and costly one.

Appointment responsibilities do not end with the transition; indeed, they never end. There are vacancies to fill throughout the administration, the result of routine turnover and the completion of term appointments. In recent years, as turnover in presidential appointments has accelerated, these vacancies have occurred more frequently. That has produced an increasing need for a full-time personnel staff function to handle ongoing appointment responsibilities.

ISSUES—VARIED AND FAR-REACHING

A quarter of a century ago, toward the end of the Eisenhower administration, a formal personnel recruiting system was established in the White House Office. That function took root and has reappeared in every succeeding administration. It is now a regular component of the modern, institutionalized presidency.

Since then some desirable changes have occurred in the way appointees are selected. Recruiting efforts have become less passive and reactive. Political and policy clearances of appointees have become more thorough and consistent. More careful checks are made into candidates' credentials and backgrounds. Much more rigorous mechanisms have been established to guard against financial conflicts of interest.

But if the appointment process has been improved, it has not yet been perfected. No more persuasive testimony of that exists than the words of those who know the process best: the ones who have been part of it in the White House and those who have studied it most closely. Their concerns, their criticisms, and their desires to see improvements in the selection and quality of presidential appointees have been the impetus for this volume. It might be well at this point to listen to what they have had to say:

> With a more systematic approach to the recruitment and selection of regulatory commissioners and a penchant for activist consumer-oriented appointees, the Kennedy regulators should all have looked and sounded like Newton Minow, conforming to the President's concept of what was in the public interest. But, of course, they did not. I can recall at least five who were considerably less than bright; at least three, including a chairman, who were pri-

marily interested in keeping everything as calm and quiet as possible both inside and outside the agency; perhaps five whose devotion to the consumer was so slight as to be undiscernible; maybe eight who showed no evidence of having had a new idea in the past quarter century.

(Dan Fenn, personnel assistant to John F. Kennedy)[6]

Generally speaking, presidents have not displayed much continued interest in the appointments process: often the process has been set up with little or no thought, and then relegated to middle level status in the White House; criteria, either on a specific selection or even of a general nature, are rarely enunciated; and presidents have frequently not insisted upon the most able appointees. The disinterest at the very highest levels of government . . . constitutes one of the major disabilities of the appointment process. No party has a corner on those problems and from time to time they appear with a stubborn regularity in every administration.

(U.S. Senate Committee on Commerce)[7]

I regretted that during the first term we had done a very poor job in the most basic business of every new administration of either party: we had failed to fill all key posts in the departments and agencies with people who were loyal to the President and his programs. Without this kind of leadership in appointive positions, there is no way for the President to make any impact on the bureaucracy.

(President Richard M. Nixon)[8]

The key to establishing some measure of managerial control over the executive branch and having any hope of making government work better is to select the right people for the many positions. Despite its obvious importance, however, the personnel selection process in government is usually conducted in a haphazard fashion and the results are generally mediocre.

(Frederic V. Malek, personnel assistant to Richard M. Nixon)[9]

I have learned in my first two and a half weeks why Abraham Lincoln and some of the older Presidents almost went home when they first got to the White House. The handling of personnel appointments, trying to get the right person in the right position at the right time is a very difficult question.

(President Jimmy Carter)[10]

A president used to call up a prospective cabinet member [and make a job offer]. The candidate would consult with his wife, call back in 24 hours and the deal was done. Now, he has to sit down, literally, with a lawyer from the transition, his own lawyer, a banker and an accountant to figure out how he can comply with all the terms.

(Edwin Meese III, counselor to Ronald Reagan)[11]

> Q. "Mr. President, it's been two months since you've taken office. . . . Is there anything you're not pleased with?
> A. "Well, if I had to say anything, it would be slowness in filling appointments. . . . And I think part of our delay has been the new rules and regulations that have been passed and imposed that make clearance of appointees take longer than it formerly did."
>
> (President Ronald Reagan)[12]

These comments suggest a conclusion that is widely shared by those who know the appointment process well: that our procedures for recruitment and confirmation are not providing the federal government in a timely way with the very best talent available to it. We believe that the time is at hand for a thorough and thoughtful reconsideration of the presidential personnel recruiting function.

The years that lie ahead will be as rich with opportunity as they are laden with danger. It is important that we have leaders creative enough to mine those opportunities and skillful and resolute enough to contain the dangers. That will happen only if the process we employ to fill the government's top offices allows us to identify and recruit the best people this country has to offer. Good appointments have always been a key to good government. But now, with our days of international isolation behind us forever and the federal government so intricately involved in the national economy, good appointments are more important than they have ever been. Too often in the past we have tolerated a presidential appointment process that was casual and careless. We can no longer afford such tolerance.

In the American political system, the appointment process is one of the busiest intersections of politics and administration. Its operations and outcomes touch on the interests of many important constituencies. In turn, the needs of each of those constituencies pose issues that affect, or should affect, the character of the appointment process. We will state some of those issues here and probe them more deeply in the chapters that follow.

Issues for the President

The president's primary concerns with appointments fall into two categories. One involves the individual qualifications and composite character of his appointments; the other is the process he employs to identify, recruit, and prepare appointees for their jobs.

These are four concerns of most importance to the president and his personnel staff when they examine appointee qualifications. The most obvious is the need for talent of the highest quality, for appointees who are able to learn and quickly master the difficult positions in which they will serve. But no president ever has the luxury of letting that qualification stand alone, unalloyed. He must also worry about the strategic and political impacts of his appointments. How will his selections be viewed by key members of Congress and by important elements in the governing coalition he will attempt to construct? Will he be able to satisfy the expectations of his loyal campaign workers for the government jobs to which they believe their efforts entitle them?

In addition to this, the collective character of his appointments must be of concern to the president. He must confront prevailing expectations that his administration will be representative of important segments of the population, that it will include visible appointments of women, blacks, Hispanics, and other representatives of religious and ethnic groups. Similarly, he will be under some pressure to adhere to the traditions of appointing a westerner to head the Interior Department, a farmer to be in charge at Agriculture, a corporate executive at Commerce, and a union member or supporter at Labor. His appointees will be judged not merely for their individual qualifications—though they will certainly be judged for that—but also for the appearance they present collectively, for the sense of presence within the government that they provide to major interests in the country.

Finally, the president will have to be concerned with the political and policy implications of important individual appointments. What will his selection of a secretary of defense indicate about the defense policy intentions of his administration, for instance? Does he have important policy objectives that will best be served by placing strong and experienced appointees in certain critical positions? How will his appointment choices affect relationships between the White House and individual departments and agencies during the course of his administration? These strategic issues are always central concerns of the presidential appointment process because they bear so directly on the accomplishment of the president's most important goals.

To satisfy all of these needs, the president requires a good staff and effective procedures for managing the appointment process. Successful performance of the personnel selection function imposes several requirements. The staff must be able to reach out beyond the White House and beyond Washington to identify people with the special talents and expertise that the job descriptions of presidential appointees require. It must then convince those people to accept the president's offer of a job in his administration, even though this may require significant personal sacrifices. Then it must move with dispatch to complete the political and conflict of interest clearances that have to be satisfied before a nomination can be formally announced.

Even then the job is not done. The smooth transition of his appointees into their new jobs is also a concern for the president because it has an effect on the quality of their performance and on the initial bonding process that should occur between them and the aims of the administration. Preparing appointees for the confirmation process, orienting them to the political environment in which they will be working, and educating them about the specific organizations and issues with which they will deal are critically important to the president. They will affect the speed with which his appointees learn their jobs and the level of understanding they develop of the underlying philosophy and policy objectives of his presidency.

Issues for New Appointees

In many ways the issues that most concern new appointees are simply the other side of those that affect the White House. Some appointees, of course, are old Washington hands, "inners and outers" who have been in and out of government many times and for whom taking on a new appointment is merely a matter of learning a new set of issues. But that is not the norm, especially not at the outset of a new administration. More typically, presidential appointees are people who have not previously worked in a presidential administration. Frequently, in fact, they have never before worked in the federal government. In many cases, they have never worked in government at all.

Fears about their ability to succeed in an unfamiliar environment is only part of the uncertainty that often colors their response to an offer to join a presidential administration. There are significant personal considerations as well. One is the impact this will have on the candidate's career in the private sector. Individuals come to the attention of White House recruiters because of the talents they have demonstrated in their work outside of government. These same talents frequently provide those individuals with a pattern of upward mobility that could be disrupted if they took time off for public service. The possibility always exists that the momentum may never be recaptured and that success in accomplishing career objectives will be more difficult if the candidate accepts a presidential appointment. That is a genuine and widespread concern among nearly everyone who faces this choice.

Equally compelling is the concern over the financial impact on appointees and their families of a sojourn in public service. Because government salaries at the highest level are not competitive with those paid to corporate executives, partners in large law firms, the leaders of special interest organizations, and even professors at the most prestigious universities, acceptance of a presidential appointment may require a reduction in salary. In some cases the reduction is substantial.

A possible decrease in salary is only one of the financial considerations that a candidate for a presidential appointment must confront. Because of the ethics laws that now regulate government employment, other financial sacrifices may be required. Some remedy must be found for any financial holding that poses a potential conflict of interest. That may require divestiture. Divestiture can be a financial double whammy because it may have to take place at a time when the holdings have not reached maximum value and because there are no provisions in the tax laws that protect appointees from heavy tax liability on their earnings at the time of divestiture.

It is also typical for new appointees moving from the private sector to lose many of the benefits they enjoyed in their employment there. Separation from private pension plans is a significant and common problem. So too is the loss of health and life insurance benefits, which are usually more ample in the private than in the public sector. And many corporate executives must give up the stock options that have been an important supplement to their salary incomes.

Relocation expenses add to this burden. The federal government provides no moving allowance for presidential appointees; they must absorb all their moving costs themselves. Those who must find a place to live in Washington quickly discover that it is one of the most expensive real estate markets in the country. The gap between their government salary and the income they are leaving behind is likely to grow even larger when housing costs are added.

One other financial concern that complicates the decision to accept a presidential appointment is the problem of what to do when the appointment is over. The normal answer for most people is to move back into the job, or into the industry, they left when they came to government. But such a move may be complicated by the "revolving door" restrictions that now exist to prevent recent government employees from contacting the agencies for which they worked as an agent for private interests.

Though significant, financial mattters are not the only issues that affect the decision to accept a presidential appointment. Presidential appointees in Washington live in the public eye. Their words and actions are matters of public importance. Their failures or indiscretions are matters of public attention. If it is not exactly life in a fishbowl, it is widely perceived to be just that. For those who are short on self-confidence or whose skin is thin, working in the glare of public observation is not a comforting prospect.

The decision to accept a presidential appointment is often a joint decision involving considerations far broader than the direct impact on the person to whom the appointment has been offered. The concerns of spouses and families weigh heavily in these decisions. A spouse may have an important job that he or she is unable or unwilling to leave. Children may be at a point in their education where uprooting is unpleasant or unwise. A family may be unhappy at the prospect of having one of its members tied down in a federal office for long hours and long weeks.

On top of all of this, there is the most obvious concern of all: the natural uncertainty that most people face when asked to take on a new and complex assignment. "Can I do this job?" is a thought that crosses the mind of nearly everyone offered a presidential appointment. It is an especially worrisome thought for someone who has never before worked for the federal government. Adding even more to the uncertainty is the knowledge that the candidate's first public appearance will be at a confirmation hearing before a committee of senators who may be anxious to explore his or her background and to probe his or her knowledge of the issues that will have to be dealt with in office. Though Senate confirmation hearings are rarely contentious, every presidential nominee has heard horror stories about them.

Some of these doubts—about the nature of the job, about life in the Washington fishbowl, and about effective performance at the confirmation hearing—could be greatly assuaged by providing the appointee with a thorough preparation for the confirmation hearing and a careful orientation to the job and to the requisites of survival in Washington. That aspect of the appointment process, however, has been overlooked in many recent presidential administrations. More typically, new appointees find themselves courted heavily up to the point at which they accept a job offer and then left to their own devices through the confirmation process and during the transition into their new jobs. A difficult time under any circumstances has been made more difficult by the failure of the White House to provide adequate support and assistance for the people it has recruited. Too often this results in a sense of isolation from the White House that is more than simply injurious to the new appointees themselves. It also undermines the respect and responsiveness the president is able to command from the people he has brought to Washington to serve in his administration.

Issues for the Senate

The Senate has a constitutional role in the appointment process—a role primarily intended to protect the public from bad appointments. Few doubt the value of the Senate's function in the process as a useful check on the president's exercise of his appointment powers. Over the years more than a few unjustifiable appointments have run aground in Senate committee rooms and on the Senate floor. But the Senate's part in the appointment process also suffers from serious flaws; in recent years three important issues have arisen in that regard.

One is the problem of inconsistency. The Senate confirmation process is managed by Senate committees. In this, as in most things, those committees operate autonomously. Each has its own set of expectations, procedures, and traditions. And each has its own reporting and paperwork requirements. This adds enormously to the burden faced by the White House and its nominees in complying with the individualized requirements of each Senate committee and in preparing for confirmation hearings.

A second problem is the occasional abuse of the confirmation process by certain senators. The Senate is a highly personal, decentralized institution. Great deference is afforded individual senators in pursuit of their own interests. One of the traditions of the Senate is that a member of a Senate committee who is not yet ready to vote on the confirmation of a nominee may place a "hold" on that nomination until the doubts have been satisfied. Not surprisingly, this is a tradition fraught with opportunities for mischief. It permits a senator who wishes to embarrass the administration, or to force it into cutting a deal with him, to use his leverage over the confirmation process for that purpose.

The third problem results from the first two. It is the problem of delay. The individual procedures and preferences of a variety of Senate committees and the occasional need to wait out interruptions imposed by individual senators both have a tendency to retard the completion of the confirmation process. This adds to the frustrations encountered by new appointees and it slows even further the already sluggish process of getting a new administration into place. The epidemic of "acting" officials due to delay in the appointment process is a major deficiency in the executive capacity of the government.

Issues for the Departments

Delays in the appointment process, whether caused at the White House or on Capitol Hill, also have an undesirable effect on executive departments and agencies. Turnover in top executive positions is a regular characteristic of our form of government, with quadrennial presidential elections and heavy reliance on noncareer executives. As a result, some measure of discontinuity is inevitable. The problems caused by that discontinuity are greatly exacerbated, however, when vacancies in top positions are allowed to persist for long periods.

Equally troublesome to the agencies and departments is the periodic appearance of a new boss whose selection was not based on any expertise in subjects within that organization's jurisdiction and who was provided no careful preparation for the position he or she was to assume. The department or agency finds itself with a new leader who, at the outset at least, is not equipped to lead. The learning curve is a long one and until it is mastered, the interests of the department are unlikely to be advanced very effectively. That is not a prospect that sits well with career employees or with the clienteles served by affected departments and agencies.

Most career officials look forward to cooperative working relationships with a new administration. But they often find themselves in need of guidance in order to orient their agencies to the policy preferences of a new president. That guidance rarely results from the typically shallow discussion of issues that occurs during presidential campaigns. Instead, it usually comes from the people appointed by the president to head their agency. When there are long delays in making that appointment, or when the appointee is someone not adequately prepared for leadership responsibilities, senior career officials lack the guidance they seek. The difficult job of redirecting the agency is delayed and becomes more difficult as the morale of the career employees declines and the enthusiasm generated by the election diminishes.

Cabinet secretaries also have a stake, a very important stake, in the operations of the appointment process. For them the critical issue is who will control the selection of their subordinates. All secretaries want to fill the critical posts in their departments with people of their own choosing. But few presidents have been willing to give their department heads carte blanche in personnel selection. Instead, this becomes a joint operation—sometimes cooperative in tone, sometimes competitive—in which department secretaries must persuade the White House to appoint people whom they support. The effort to do this is a constant struggle, and the allocation of control over the appointment process is therefore a common issue of concern for cabinet secretaries.

Issues for Private Sector Leaders

Those who lead organizations in the private sector (corporations, communications media, labor unions, law firms, universities, interest groups) obviously have a primary interest in the health and prosperity of their own organizations. When the president of the United States plucks away one of their talented employees to serve in his administration, that is a problem for them, or so they often perceive it. They have trained those employees and nurtured them up through the organizational hierarchy and now they are losing them right in the midst of their most creative years.

Not surprisingly, there have been many cases in which private sector employers have actively discouraged their employees from accepting a presidential appointment. Even when not actively discouraging this, employers have done little to facilitate it or to find ways to allow their best employees to integrate periods of public service into the normal progress of their private careers.

Yet, when accomplished with sensitivity to the problem of conflict of interest, this kind of personnel interchange between the private and public sectors can be beneficial to both. It allows those whose worklives are directly affected by government policies to see government from the inside and to acquire an understanding of the breadth of perspectives that inform and inspire public policy. It also allows those who are familiar with government actions from the receiving end to carry that perspective with them into the public sector, where it is too often absent. Mutual understanding can result from this particular kind of "inning and outing," and neither the public nor the private sector has gained much from their failure to encourage and facilitate it more effectively.

Issues in the Public Interest

The ultimate objective of the appointment process is the selection of leaders who will serve the public with competence, integrity, and creativity. Public service means just that: service to the public. The final and most important test of the success of the appointment process is the extent to which it serves the public interest. If it fails to staff the leading positions in the federal government with able people, if those people are not fair and open minded in their judgments, or if they abuse the public trust for private gain, then the appointment process has failed—regardless of whose special interests it serves well.

It is precisely because of widespread concern with this last point that this study was initiated. The public interest has not been well served by the appointment process as it has operated in recent presidential administrations. Too many people lacking talents appropriate for the complexity of their jobs have found their way into high-level federal positions. Too little has been done to identify untapped sources of administrative talent or to recruit effectively from those sources outside the government that are already well known. The appointment process has not provided American presidents with the kind of support they need to construct their administrations in a wise and timely fashion. This study was undertaken in the faith that we can do better than this and in the belief that we must.

In short, we believe it is imperative—and possible—to develop solutions to many of the problems identified here. In this report we have undertaken to begin that process. At a minimum, we hope our efforts to examine and respond to these problems will generate a national dialogue leading to the establishment of a presidential appointment process fully adequate to the requirements of good government in the United States.

NOTES

1. Quoted in Richard M. Nixon, *RN: The Memoirs of Richard Nixon*, Vol. I (New York: Warner Books, 1978), p. 643.
2. James M. Landis, *Report on Regulatory Agencies to the President-Elect*, 1960. (Unpublished), p. 66.
3. John Gardner, *No Easy Victories* (New York: Harper & Row, 1968), p. 6.
4. Jacob E. Cooke, ed., *The Federalist*, no. 76 (Cleveland, Ohio: Meridian Books, 1961), p. 513.
5. G. Calvin Mackenzie, "The Paradox of Presidential Personnel Management," in Hugh Heclo and Lester M. Salamon, eds., *The Illusion of Presidential Government* (Boulder: Westview Press, 1981), p. 117.
6. Dan H. Fenn, Jr., "Dilemmas for the Regulator," *California Management Review* 16 (1974): 89.
7. U.S. Senate, Committee on Commerce, *The Regulatory Appointments Process* (Washington, D.C.: U.S. Government Printing Office, 1977), p. 145.
8. Nixon, Vol. II, p. 284.
9. Frederic V. Malek, *Washington's Hidden Tragedy* (New York: Free Press, 1978), p. 63.
10. Jimmy Carter, Presidential Press Conference, February 8, 1977.
11. Quoted in "Ethics Law Makes The Choice That Much Harder," *New York Times*, December 14, 1980.
12. *Washington Post*, March 28, 1981.

Chapter 2

DEVELOPMENT OF THE MODERN APPOINTMENT PROCESS

We have had presidential appointments since the beginning of our history as a republic. For most of that time, however, we have not had a presidential appointment process. If by "process" we mean a consistent, thoughtfully developed set of procedures, we can say that a presidential appointment process has existed for only the past twenty-five years.

Even in this most recent period, however, we have seen more than a few lapses in professionalism, political sensitivity, and administrative sophistication in the management of the appointment process. We have come a long way from the days when a president, needing to fill a vacancy in his administration, would telephone the leader of his political party and ask, "Who have you got?" But the record of the past few decades also indicates that we haven't come as far from that day as we should have. Modernization of the presidential appointment process began in the period since World War II. We have made a start toward the establishment of an effective personnel selection operation in the White House. But it is only a start. There are gains still to be consolidated and lessons still to be learned.

Because so much of the relevant history of the appointment process has occurred in the past twenty-five years, that is the principal emphasis of this chapter.[1] In exploring this history we try to emphasize those aspects of the development of the presidential appointment process that mark genuine turning points and are important contributions to the manner in which presidential appointees are selected.

THE HISTORICAL EXPERIENCE

The "Old Days"

If those who had participated in the selection of presidential appointees in our earliest administrations could have revisited Washington in the third and fourth decades of this century, they might have observed practices that would have looked familiar to them. There were a few more offices to fill, to be sure, and political parties had become more prominent than they had known them to be, but for the most part, the selection of presidential appointees had not changed much over the first 150 years of our history.

It was still the case that vacancies were filled with little advance planning, without a broad or systematic search for talented candidates, and with only the most casual assessment of the backgrounds and integrity of those who were nominated. Often, the appointee selection process was pigeonholed under "politics" rather than "administration." In the years when the president lacked any significant staff support, the personnel function was typically controlled by his political party. Even when the president himself took an active role in selecting his own cabinet, he was often hemmed in by the need to compose a cabinet that balanced the competing factions of his own party. Other appointees, below the cabinet level, were usually suggested to the president by party leaders, personal acquaintances, or members of Congress. Since the president had few alternative sources and little time or staff capability to drum them up, he usually had little choice in staffing his administration but to rely on the political sources most familiar to him.

Not surprisingly, this made for some odd bedfellows. Presidents in the nineteenth and early twentieth centuries often presided over cabinets and administrations in which comity and cooperation were scarce commodities. Because the selection of their appointees had followed from no consensual definition of a presidential philosophy or approach to government management, appointees were often ill suited to that task. And because they realized that their appointments had resulted not from the personal preferences of the president himself but rather from the recommendations of party leaders, their loyalty to the president's objectives and their responsiveness to his orders were anything but ensured. Appointment decisions vibrated to the rhythms of political exigency; administrative considerations rarely intervened.

Only in the 1930s, when the presidency began to acquire a formal staff, did some hope develop for fuller presidential control over the appointment process. In Franklin Roosevelt's administration, for the first time, an individual was designated to handle personnel matters. This did little to alter the role of partisan politics in this process, for the principal duty of this assistant was to serve as the president's liaison to his party's national committee and to work with the committee in verifying the political pedigree of the president's appointees. It was a step toward improved presidential control over the appointment process, but it was a short one indeed.

The Beginnings of Modernization

The Truman White House was the first to have a staff member who spent the bulk of his time working on personnel matters. That man was Donald Dawson, and while the personnel functions he performed were largely routine, his concentration on them marked a new level of emphasis on personnel matters. Dawson had a small clerical staff who helped him with the processing of job solicitations, endorsements, and clearances on appointments. But, like his predecessors in the previous administration, a good deal of his time was spent in contact with the Democratic National Committee and with state, local, and congressional party leaders.

In the last two years of the Truman administration, without public attention and without much real impact on President Truman's appointments, some members of his staff began to study the appointment process more thoughtfully than had ever before been the case. The impetus for this came from Dawson and a lower level White House aide named Martin Friedman, who had gained professional personnel experience as a career civilian in the Pentagon. They called in a consultant and together formed a group composed of talented, mostly young, assistant secretaries to look at the problems of presidential personnel selection. This "little cabinet" group, as it came to be known, identified two important steps that might be taken to improve the effectiveness of the appointment process and the quality of its products.

First, it pointed out the president's need for a reliable catalogue of talented individuals, independent of party patronage lists, from which he could draw in filling the important posts in his administration. This was regarded as a special need of the Truman administration, as it became harder and harder after 1950 to recruit people from the private sector into what was widely perceived as a lame duck administration. So the little cabinet group went ahead on its own to look at individuals already working within the government and to identify those who might be appointed to positions of higher responsibility as those positions became vacant in Truman's final years in the White House.

Equally important, in the view of this group, was a better understanding of the character and requirements of the positions that were filled by presidential appointment. How, after all, could a wise appointment be made if the talents of the appointee were not matched up with the demands of the job? But, historically, there had been no effort to do that in any systematic way. In response, the little cabinet group set out to draw up a list of important appointive positions and to write careful job descriptions for each.

This effort came too late in his administration to have much impact on Harry Truman's presidential appointments, but in the development of the appointment process, it was significant in two ways. First, it marked the initial identification of the president's need for a personnel support function that is something more than an extension of the patronage operations of the national parties. Second, it suggested that one prerequisite to establishing that kind of independent personnel apparatus was to free the president from his reliance on his party for the names of candidates well qualified to serve in his administration. Though barely made operational at the time of their initiation, these ideas would later loom large in the development of the appointment process.

Dwight D. Eisenhower came to office in 1953 committed to improving the quality of management in the White House. As a high-ranking military officer he had had considerable contact with the White House over the years, and he was convinced that the work of the place "could be better systematized than it had been during the years I had observed it."[2]

One of the areas in which this effort was most pronounced was in the handling of presidential appointments. Before Eisenhower took office, one of his supporters commissioned a New York consulting firm to study a president's appointment responsibilities and to identify the major offices that a new chief executive would have to fill.

This study produced a list of 915 important positions to which Eisenhower could make appointments. It marked the first time that any president had begun his term with a clear sense of the scope and character of his appointment responsibilities.

President Eisenhower had a strong distaste for personnel matters. He often noted in his diary that patronage concerns were one of the great plagues of his administration and the single concern most likely to prevent him from keeping his temper under control. His tendency then was to delegate responsibility for the appointment process to members of his White House staff. During his time with the administration, Sherman Adams was the major-domo of this process. But even he was too busy to tend to the day-to-day details of the process, and he and the president soon came to recognize the benefits of establishing a full-time staff within the White House to oversee the appointment process.

Early in Eisenhower's first term, the administration established the position of special assistant for executive appointments. This position was held by several people during the course of the administration, but its duties remained essentially unchanged. The special assistant was the manager of the appointment process. He did not choose the administration's appointees, but he administered the paperwork and served as liaison with the Republican National Committee, state and local party officials, and members of Congress. The special assistant and his staff were able, through their efforts to simplify the president's personnel choices by filtering through the lists of candidates presented to the White House, to identify those with the strongest substantive qualifications and the fewest political liabilities.

Because of the concern with security risks that was so prevalent during the early years of the Eisenhower presidency, this administration became the first to require that all its potential appointees be subjected to a Federal Bureau of Investigation background check before their nominations were sent forward to the Senate. This practice quickly became precedent and has been followed by every subsequent administration. These background checks, like the other details of the appointment process, were managed by the personnel staff under the direction of the special assistant for executive appointments.

Because it was the first Republican administration in twenty years—years of enormous growth in the scope of government activity and in the size of the federal establishment—the Eisenhower presidency felt a strong need to wrest control of the government from the Democrats who had been running it for two decades. To do that required a vigorous exercise of the appointment power. Competent Eisenhower loyalists had to be identified and appointed to positions where they could impose the president's political philosophy on the operations of the government.

It was this desire more than anything that accounts for the heightened level of attention given to personnel matters in the Eisenhower White House. More staff members were assigned to personnel and the appointment process was managed more carefully than in any previous administration. But, in reality, the dynamics of the appointment process had not changed very much from earlier years. President Eisenhower was little involved in appointments; most of his appointment authority was, in fact, exercised by his senior staff. The appointment process was still treated largely as part of a party patronage operation. In the first term, especially, the Republican National Committee was given a major role in identifying and approving candidates for presidential appointments, and no significant effort was developed to permit the White House to identify potential appointees beyond those names that came in unsolicited. The emphasis remained, as it had in earlier administrations, on finding jobs for people, not on finding people for jobs. The Eisenhower administration made improvements in the management of the appointment process, but it did not shift the fundamental character of that process very far from its traditional roots. That shift began in the Kennedy administration.

The Appointment Process Redefined

Like most twentieth century presidents, John Kennedy was unprepared to handle the burden of appointments that fell on him after his election. He had been unwilling during the campaign to divert any resources to establish a staff to prepare for the transition in the event of a victory. As a result, he and his close aides were forced to jury-rig a transition personnel operation in a very short time. What they created came to be called the "Talent Hunt." It was a loosely organized, multicentered, emergency operation employing some of the best people from the campaign.

The Talent Hunt had two principal components. One focused on the president-elect's political obligations and spent much of its time deciding which of the people who had helped Kennedy win election should be awarded jobs in his administration. The other focused on the jobs themselves. It began by trying to identify the most important of the positions the president would have to fill. This turned out to be no easy task since no listing of these positions was readily available and the one list that was procured from a congressional committee provided little information about the nature of these positions and the appropriate skills and experience for the people appointed to fill them. This was a repeat of the frustration every new administration had encountered in trying to get a handle on the kinds of jobs it would have to fill.

The Kennedy Talent Hunt finished its top priority appointment work shortly after the inauguration and its members scattered to their own jobs in the new administration. It soon became apparent, however, that the appointment process involved more than merely filling a group of jobs at the outset of the administration. Because of fixed-term appointments and routine turnover, there were always vacancies to fill and, thus, a need for some kind of permanent personnel support operation in the White House. Kennedy had assigned responsibility for personnel matters to Ralph Dungan, a member of his staff. But Dungan had other responsibilities as well and lacked the time to give personnel the full attention it required. Therefore, he hired Dan Fenn of the Harvard Business School faculty to join the White House staff and take over the day-to-day management of the personnel function. Fenn was also asked to take an objective look at the appointment process and to recommend whatever improvements he thought desirable.

Fenn found much to change. His most significant concern, however, was with the narrow range of sources on which presidents had traditionally relied to find candidates for appointments in their administrations. Fenn gave this traditional system a label that has become part of the lore of the appointment process: The BOGSAT system. BOGSAT means a "bunch of guys sitting around a table" asking each other "Whom do you know?" It was, in Fenn's view, an unsophisticated way to select the nation's top administrative officers.

Fenn and his staff set out to develop a better approach. Their sense was that an effective appointment process rested on three pillars. The first was a clear understanding of the kinds of jobs they had to fill. Before they could identify good candidates they had to have penetrating and reliable job descriptions. That seems so obvious as to hardly bear mentioning, but, as this narrative has suggested, most administrations before this time had undertaken their appointment duties without a clear sense of what they were looking for.

The second element that Fenn sought to establish was an outreach capability. He quickly came to realize that the sample of people who came to the president's attention through normal, largely political, channels was much too narrow to provide the base of talented appointees upon which the success of the administration would heavily rely. Furthermore, those who sought presidential appointments often lacked the technical skills and experience necessary to perform many of the important jobs a president has to fill. If an administration relied on only those candidates who bubbled up through party channels or who volunteered their services, two undesirable consequences would ensue. One is that many of the most talented people in the country would simply never find their way into the public service because there was no mechanism for identifying or recruiting them. The other is that the president would often find himself with little recourse but to appoint candidates suggested to him—or, often, forced upon him—by other politicians in his party. Without an independent recruiting capability of his own, he would have few alternatives to candidates emerging from those sources. Hence, the development of such a capability was important not merely to provide a better range of potential appointees from which to choose but also to afford the president greater mastery over the political forces that play so heavily upon the appointment process.

The third component of Fenn's approach was necessitated by the second. If a president were to reach out beyond the traditional political sources for his appointees, he would need some reliable people to help him judge the qualifications of those potential appointees. In most cases, the people he would be seeking would be strangers to him and he would naturally be uncomfortable in appointing them to high office without some independent assessment of their abilities. What this required was the help of some well-positioned people throughout the country whose judgment and candor were trusted by the White House and who could be called upon to provide assessments of candidates being considered for appointment. This was not a perfect substitute for direct acquaintance with these candidates, but it would be significantly better than nothing at all.

The operation that Fenn set up sought to establish each of these components as a regular part of the White House appointment process. He began by expanding his staff to six people and dividing responsibilities among them. The selection of people to fill the largely honorific positions on presidential boards and commissions–still very much a patronage function–was separated from the more important responsibility of recruiting appointees to serve in line positions in the executive branch. Much effort was concentrated by Fenn and the professionals on his staff in trying to define the requirements for the jobs they had to fill. This often put them in contact with people in the appropriate agencies and with others, both in and out of government, who could help them identify the character of a particular job and define the special skills and knowledge that would be most needed at that time by the person they would select to fill it.

Fenn also spent some of this time in the White House trying to develop a talent bank of individuals qualified for presidential appointments. The idea was to have a readily available roster from which the personnel staff could draw in generating names of candidates to fill vacant positions. Though it was used with some success, the talent bank was not a simple operation to administer. Developing and managing a talent bank adequate to the needs of the White House was a major logistical task for a small personnel staff. It was also very hard to keep information in the talent bank up to date. Though there was a constant effort to make this approach work, it was never quite as successful as its advocates would have liked.

More successful, in the view of the Kennedy personnel people, was their attempt to create a living source of potential appointees in the form of what came to be known as the "contact network." Fenn drew on the assistance of the Brookings Institution and others to help him establish a list of several hundred national leaders in industry, labor, state government, universities, and other fields of endeavor upon whom the White House could call when it needed help in identifying potential appointees. Persons on the contact list would be used both to suggest candidates and to serve as references for those suggested by others. Over time, the contact list became more sophisticated and grew into several lists: a general list of reliable people with a wide circle of acquaintances and a series of specialized lists relevant to the job search in particular fields.

The contact network idea was heavily used by the Kennedy administration as a mechanism for circumventing the normal political channels from which candidates for appointments emerged. The network required regular maintenance. As the personnel staff was able to evaluate the quality of advice it received from people in the network, it purged some from the lists and relied more heavily on others. The network had a dynamic quality, changing constantly as the White House reassessed its needs.

That this was not a flawless source of reliable information is not surprising, for personnel selection is hard to perfect. It was, however, an important turning point in the development of the appointment process because it marked the first time that a president had a personnel support system that provided him with an independent recruiting capability, with the capacity—and the freedom—to conduct a genuine national talent search for his own administration.

This was not, nor was it intended to be, a depoliticization of the appointment process. No one in the Kennedy White House seriously thought that the politics could ever be taken out of the process of filling the top jobs in an administration. What was intended here was the development of a personnel operation that permitted the president to prevail more often in the political conflict over these positions. With an independent recruiting capability the president could often find better qualified candidates than those recommended to him by his party, by members of Congress, and by the leaders of interest groups. If he was unhappy with their recommendations, he had alternatives. He could come up with candidates who were better than theirs. And, because the president alone would be their patron, he could expect a higher degree of loyalty and responsiveness from appointees recruited through the White House personnel staff than from those recommended to him from other sources.

For all of its efforts to improve the quality of presidential personnel selection, the personnel operation established during the Kennedy years never worked as well as it might have. A principal reason for that was President Kennedy's inconsistency in using it. Kennedy did not have a very active interest in personnel matters. He intervened occasionally in individual cases, but he paid little attention to the day-to-day operation of the appointment process. Indeed, he often circumvented that process entirely by selecting appointees without using the process that Fenn had set up.

The impact of Kennedy's inconsistency was that the personnel operation was never able to establish the visibility or legitimacy necessary to the genuine and effective management of the appointment process. Washington's sharpest politicians quickly came to realize that it was possible to circumvent the formal personnel operation and thus get their recommendations to the president directly before Fenn and his staff had geared up for their independent national search. Although it was obviously Kennedy's choice to permit this, it undermined much of the potential value that he might have derived from the much improved appointment procedures that Fenn and his staff had developed.

The administration of Lyndon Johnson provides an interesting contrast. Unlike Kennedy, Johnson took a strong personal interest in appointment decisions. Although his reliance on the personnel staff was not perfect, he was much more willing to use it as a buffer to ward off intrusions from those who wanted to exercise influence on his appointment decisions.

Johnson took the unusual step of designating John Macy as head of the personnel selection operation in the White House. It was unusual because Macy simultaneously served as chairman of the Civil Service Commission and as the president's chief adviser on all personnel matters. The practice of having the same person heading the civil service and managing the process of noncareer personnel selection was worrisome to many students of public administration. It was subsequently prohibited under provisions of the Civil Service Reform Act of 1978. But during the mid-1960s, it did give John Macy considerable visibility in his work on presidential appointments—visibility that Johnson often used to his advantage by telling job seekers and their patrons that, as much as he'd like to appoint them, he couldn't do so because Macy insisted that appointments be based on merit and had come up with a sterling candidate of his own. It was an approach that could only have been used by a president who took an active part in the appointment process and who was willing to protect the position of his personnel staff as managers of that process.

Macy continued many of the developments in personnel selection that had been instituted in the previous administration. He also brought a new emphasis on professionalism and administrative efficiency to this function. He enlarged the personnel staff and further divided the labor of its members. Specific areas of responsibility were assigned to individual members of the staff so that one group dealt wih domestic appointments and another with those in foreign affairs. Macy believed that these constituted quite different kinds of executive recruiting and he wanted his staff to be well versed in the special requirements of the areas in which they worked.

Macy also introduced automated data processing into the appointment process. He picked up on the idea of a talent bank, originated by Dan Fenn, and greatly expanded the list of potential candidates he inherited. By the end of the Johnson administration there were approximately 30,000 names contained in the talent bank. These were cross-referenced by skills and background characteristics to permit appropriate candidates to be identified for particular job vacancies. Computers were used for the first time to permit ready access to this information.

Macy also shared Fenn's belief in the importance of defining job requirements before beginning a personnel search. This, too, was a function developed more fully in the Johnson administration than it ever had been previously. Macy staffed the White House personnel office with people broadly experienced in the federal government, especially those who had worked in the Budget Bureau or the Civil Service Commission, where they would have become intimately familiar with the characteristics of a wide range of federal jobs. He and his staff spent a good deal of their time developing what they called "position profiles." These were based on current information about each office and were updated whenever it became vacant to account for short-term changes in the kinds of skills or experience a particular position might require. Only after this was completed did a personnel search begin in earnest.

Macy was a strong supporter of the need for the White House to develop its own executive recruitment capability. He worked closely with the president in tripling the size of the list of contacts inherited from Kennedy. The list was also reshaped to include a number of people with whom Lyndon Johnson was personally familiar and in whose judgment he had great confidence. The talent bank and the contact network were used in tandem to identify and recruit many of Johnson's appointees.

During the Johnson administration the development of the personnel staff took a long step forward. This was because the president himself put great emphasis on the work of that staff. Though he sometimes made appointment decisions without regard to the normal personnel selection procedures, he was consistent in maintaining the appearance of relying on the personnel staff. Those who wanted to influence his appointment decisions quickly got the message that their contact point for this was the personnel staff and that efforts to evade the established personnel selection procedures would be difficult to pull off. This focused more attention on the White House personnel staff than had ever before been the case and significantly strengthened its role at the hub of the appointment process.

The Appointment Process in Place: Variations on a Theme

The appointment process that emerged in the Kennedy and Johnson administrations had several prominent characteristics that have been adopted by each subsequent administration. These include a full-time personnel staff as part of the White House Office, an effort to maintain a recruiting capability independent of the president's political party, and adherence to a set of routine procedures for examining the background, integrity, competence, and political acceptability of potential appointees.

Since 1968, however, we have seen some variations on these persistent themes. The appointment process in each administration has reflected the unique predisposition of each president and the differing perspectives of their top assistants for personnel. Sometimes in fact, variations have occurred during the course of a single administration as efforts were made to repair appointment procedures that simply weren't working. The Nixon administration illustrates this.

Richard Nixon had almost no interest in personnel matters. He happily delegated this responsibility to members of his staff and participated in appointment decisions only for positions at the very top levels. Because of this disinterest and because the Nixon personnel aides had had little contact with their counterparts in previous administrations, personnel selection during the transition and through 1969 reflected few of the developments that had occurred in the appointment process in the previous decade. The Nixon personnel staff essentially started from scratch in determining how to select its appointees.

It didn't do very well, at least not in the view of those who were closest to the president. The appointment process was slow and cumbersome, no systematic outreach procedures had been developed, the management needs of the president were often a low-level consideration in appointment decisions, and far too many appointees were people who did not agree with the president on important substantive matters.

Given the lack of attention paid to personnel matters by the president and his senior staff, it is not surprising that this happened. Nor is it surprising that a new administration should find its personnel selection efforts unhinged from the lessons of the past. When the Nixon administration came into office, no written records remained from the personnel staff of any previous administration. These records are regarded as part of each president's "papers," and they leave the White House when he does. Since there are no career people working on presidential appointments, no one is around to instruct a new administration on what its predecessors did or to warn it of the pitfalls encountered in the past. There is no "institutional memory" to carry the accumulated knowledge of the appointment process from one administration to the next.

This problem can be overcome somewhat through discussions during the transition between relevant staff members in succeeding administrations. This is rarely an effective substitute, however. New administrations are often anxious to dissociate themselves from their predecessors, not to continue their work. Elections often leave bitter feelings that complicate friendly relations during the transition. And, of course, the old administration—especially if it has been defeated by the new—is often not particularly anxious to lend assistance to its successor.

The effect of the absence of any reliable institutional memory in the appointment process is that administrations often repeat the mistakes of the past and take an unnecessarily long time to get their operation up to speed in order to fill the large number of vacancies that occur during the transition period. The Nixon administration suffered both of those afflictions; so too did the Carter and Reagan administrations later on.

By 1970, members of Richard Nixon's senior White House staff had come to recognize some of the flaws in their own procedures for selecting high-level appointees. Frederic V. Malek was called in from his management position in the Department of Health, Education and Welfare to study the personnel staff and to recommend improvements. This he did in a report submitted to the senior staff in December 1970. Ironically, the report recommended the establishment of personnel management procedures that in many ways resembled those developed in the two preceding administrations: centralization of the appointment process in the White House, clearer specification of selection criteria, a more explicit clearance process, and a much more aggressive recruiting effort.

Malek himself was hired to take over the personnel staff in 1971, and he did so with vigor. Acting on his own recommendations, he created what was formally known as the White House Personnel Operation (WHPO). The WHPO followed a number of the patterns established by Fenn and Macy, but it operated at a much higher level of intensity. The staff was considerably larger than in previous administrations, which permitted far greater specialization. Staff members were assigned responsibilities either for specific types of appointments (i.e., regulatory commissions, health and welfare), or they were given other personnel management responsibilities (evaluating current appointees, overseeing congressional clearance, etc.). The WHPO also employed professional executive recruiters for the first time. These were people with limited experience in government but extensive experience as "headhunters" in the private sector. This was part of Malek's effort to expand his staff's recruitment capabilities.

The WHPO also developed the most systematic evaluation system ever employed for rating potential appointees, and it broadened its scope of operations to include virtually all noncareer positions in the federal government. There was a firm commitment here to solidify White House control over all of the personnel positions not protected by civil service regulations. In the Nixon administration, for the first time, the desire to do this was matched by the resources necessary to carry it out.

The intensity that Malek generated in the WHPO did not last much beyond the 1972 elections. There were several reasons for this. One was the departure of Malek from the WHPO to the Office of Management and Budget. Though he continued to keep an eye on the personnel operation, day-to-day management fell into other, less assertive, hands. During this time, the expansiveness of the personnel operation seemed to get out of control as it tried to push its influence beyond the normal range of presidential appointments into a large number of other personnel decisions throughout the executive branch. The excesses of some of the members of the WHPO in trespassing beyond the limits of propriety—and, in some cases, beyond the law—in trying to control career assignments provoked controversy in the press and investigations in Congress. This forced the WHPO to retreat from some of its boldest intentions. Finally, Watergate intervened. The driving thrust of the WHPO, to impose the president's own philosophical preferences and management needs on the executive branch, increasingly gave way to more immediate concerns. In personnel matters, as in everything else, it became necessary for the administration to tend to its political fences, especially in its relations with Congress, to try to ensure the survival of the Nixon presidency.

It was immediately apparent, upon his assumption of the presidency, that Gerald Ford would be one of those presidents who take an active interest in the appointment process. It was good that he did, for his administration faced the toughest recruiting challenges in the twentieth century. In the aftermath of Watergate the reputation of the public service was in substantial decline. This made it hard to attract talented people from outside the government. Ford's problems were compounded by the short time between his accession to office and the next presidential election. People who joined his administration could not be certain that their tenure in Washington would be long enough to justify the interruption of their careers in the private sector. Ford's personal willingness to participate actively in the appointment process added some weight to his administration's recruitment efforts and helped to prevent a tough situation from becoming a disaster.

A principal objective of Ford's personnel staff, first under William Walker and later under Douglas Bennett, was to correct the reputation for aggressiveness and insensitivity that had emerged in the latter days of the Nixon administration. This began with a name change: The White House Personnel Operation became the Presidential Personnel Office. But it was also reflected in a reduction in the size of the personnel operation and a much narrower focus of activities, with concentration almost solely on those positions traditionally viewed as presidential appointments. Though it was somewhat larger and more specialized, in most other ways the Ford appointment process closely resembled the model developed by Fenn and Macy.

After the election of Jimmy Carter in 1976, the problems of transition personnel selection were once again amply illustrated. Like Kennedy and Nixon before him, Carter inherited empty filing cabinets. Since he had just beaten Gerald Ford by a narrow margin in a hard-fought campaign, communications between the two men's staffs were strained and not terribly productive. Carter, therefore, went back to the drawing board to design his own set of appointment procedures.

There was a new element in the Carter transition, however. He was the first president to begin formal planning for his administration before the election. Starting in the summer of 1976, a small staff was set up in Atlanta to get a head start on some transition concerns, especially personnel. Working under the direction of Jack Watson, this group began to identify the important positions that Carter would fill if elected and to establish lists of people who might be appropriate candidates to fill those positions. By election day, the project was well advanced and it was expanded and transformed into what became known as the Talent Inventory Program (TIP). TIP was intended to serve as the first step in a nationwide recruiting effort by providing a comprehensive inventory of potential appointees and indicating the kinds of positions for which their qualifications recommended them.

As good an idea as this early start was, much of it was wasted by the Carter staff. After the election a power struggle ensued between the essentially nonpolitical approach of the Watson staff and TIP on the one hand and the politicians who had managed Carter's campaign on the other. The result was that no central coordinating mechanism emerged to manage the appointment process, and much of the work done by TIP was simply disregarded. A personnel staff was eventually established in the White House, but its ability to control the appointment process was undermined by a confused mandate.

Carter had made it clear early in the transition that he intended to have a "cabinet government"—that he would select strong managers to run the departments and then give them substantial autonomy in selecting their own subordinates. Naturally, the people appointed to his cabinet took him seriously. On the other hand, he wanted his personnel staff to take an active part in recruiting and in ensuring that his appointees were well qualified and free of conflict of interest. It was not clear where final authority resided, and what emerged was a system known as "mutual veto." In theory this meant that the White House and the departments would participate jointly in personnel selection and that either could veto a candidate it thought unacceptable. In reality the personnel staff's veto was rarely exercised.

The effect of this was to decentralize appointment decisions in a way that hadn't occurred at least since the first year of the Nixon administration and perhaps not since the early days of Eisenhower's first term. This resulted in broad inconsistencies in the character and quality of Carter's appointments. In some departments aggressive outreach efforts were undertaken and appointees were recruited from sources never before effectively tapped for presidential appointments. In other departments it was politics as usual as the "old boy" network was employed to select people whose principal qualifications were friendship with and loyalty to department secretaries and agency heads. The White House personnel staff lacked the resources and the visible presidential support to do anything about this. Only toward the end of the Carter administration, under the leadership of Arnie Miller, were vigorous efforts made to correct those deficiencies.

Before it had been in office many months, the Carter administration began to be criticized for the slow pace with which it was filling positions in the executive branch. A number of vacancies remained unfilled even into the late spring. It is not a simple matter to account for this, especially since there is a tendency to assume that the administration's early start should have hastened the staffing process. Part of the problem was the uncertainty of responsibility and the decentralization of the process described above. Another is the rigorous emphasis that the president wanted placed on security and conflict of interest investigations—time-consuming matters that inevitably lengthened the appointment process. Also a factor was the natural difficulty in trying to recruit an entire presidential administration at the same time that a personnel staff was being hired and appointment procedures were being worked out. The Carter administration learned, as others had before it, that it is no simple matter to construct a sound personnel selection system at precisely the time that system is under peak load.

Finally, the Carter personnel effort suffered from the president's distance from the process. His early interest faded quickly as other substantive concerns captured his attention. Without his intervention and support the White House personnel staff lacked the clout necessary to drive the appointment process along at a more rapid rate. The president alone had the power to referee the disputes and clarify the confusion that retarded the emplacement of his administration. No one else could fill the leadership vacuum created by his failure to do that.

The most recent personnel illustration, in the Reagan administration, demonstrates yet another variant on some of the familiar characteristics of the post–World War II appointment process. The Reagan experience reveals much of what is valuable and a good deal of what remains troublesome in the development of the appointment process. It is especially revealing because it provides us with a very clear case of what the appointment process looks like when it is run by an administration committed to managing it effectively and a president willing to play an active role in appointment decisions.

Ronald Reagan, like his predecessor, began before the presidential election to plan for the task of staffing an administration. This planning was recommended by Edwin Meese and carried out by a small staff under the direction of E. Pendleton James. James was a professional executive recruiter with previous experience as a headhunter in the administration of Richard Nixon. He carried with him to the Reagan administration a philosophy that had been in vogue in the Nixon years: that in order to impose his own sense of policy direction on the executive branch, the president had to maximize the leverage available to him in his appointment powers. If he failed to appoint people who shared his objectives and who possessed the talents necessary to implement them, a president was unlikely to have much impact on the administrative process.[3]

The Reagan planning effort did many of the things that had been attempted four years earlier. It was more successful, however, in avoiding some of the errors of the Carter effort. For one thing, the focus of the administration's personnel selection efforts remained consistent. From the earliest planning stages through the transition and for most of the first year and a half of the Reagan presidency, Pendleton James was in charge of the day-to-day management of the appointment process. A changing cast of characters participated in this along the way, but James maintained a steady presence throughout. While there was no shortage of internal debate over particular appointments, there was never much confusion over how the appointment process was structured or about the formal lines of responsibility it followed.

The Reagan personnel effort further benefited from the president's visible support for the process and from the appearance of his active participation in it. It was widely reported that he made the final decision on all important appointments in the transition and during the first year. This proved to be an effective deterrent to those in the departments and agencies and in Congress who might try to wrest control of appointment decisions away from the White House. It is one thing to attempt that when low-level White House staff members are making appointment decisions; it is quite another when those decisions are being made in the Oval Office.

But even with all this, the Reagan administration encountered more than its share of frustration and criticism in staffing its top positions. Principal among these was the length of time it took to get the administration fully in place. What had seemed only an aberration in 1977 now seemed a haunting irony: the two administrations that had started earlier than any others in our history to prepare for the appointment responsibilities of the transition had taken longer than any of the others to carry out those responsibilities.

Accounting for this in the Reagan administration was no simpler than it had been four years earlier. Much of the blame was placed on a more stringent set of disclosure and conflict of interest requirements enacted by Congress in 1978. That, no doubt, had some impact on the pace at which appointments proceeded. If that is a factor, however, it is certainly not the sole one in accounting for the difficulty the last two presidents have experienced in getting their administrations into place.

There is something more fundamental causing this problem. Several trends have converged in recent years to complicate the appointment process, especially at the outset of a new administration. One of these is simply that government has grown and there are more positions to fill than ever before. Another is that the political parties no longer serve as the clearinghouses on patronage requests. Instead of going through party channels to apply for a political job with a new administration, applications now go directly to the president-elect. This creates an enormous and politically delicate logistical problem at a time when a new administration is unlikely to be well equipped to handle it.

Further affecting this process is the heavy emphasis that has been placed on ethical and conflict of interest considerations in the last two decades, but especially in the years since Watergate. Though the benefits of these considerations are much to be desired, there is no question that they introduce some new and complicating factors into the appointment process. There is evidence that they make recruiting more difficult because they raise the stakes, and in some cases the financial costs, of a sojourn in public service. They also require much more elaborate investigation and disclosure procedures which delay the completion of the selection process.

Finally, and perhaps most importantly, the pace of the appointment process has been affected by the desire of most recent administrations to do a better job of staffing their administrations than has historically been the case. The importance of personnel selection, especially at the outset of a new administration, is now widely recognized. The need to exercise the appointment power with care and wisdom has become the conventional view among recent presidential administrations. The simple fact is that it takes more time to select appointees carefully than to do so haphazardly.

It is probably the case, therefore, that care and speed cannot always be coincident. In the way the appointment process is now operated, it may not be possible for a new administration to recruit aggressively, choose deliberately, carry out clearances diligently, and still move as quickly as all of its critics might wish through the many hundreds of positions that have to be filled.

Improvement is not likely to come through simple exhortations about the importance of a smooth and rapid transition. What is needed instead are fundamental changes in the appointment process—changes that permit a presidential administration to cope effectively with its personnel responsibilities.

SUMMARY

There is much to admire in the changes that have taken place in the appointment process in the past twenty-five years. Significant improvements have been made in the resources, techniques, and procedures employed by recent presidents to find able people to staff the top jobs in their administrations. Among these, the most important are:

- the apparent institutionalization of a personnel staff in the White House Office to manage the appointment process;
- the evolution of coherent and systematic procedures for evaluating the qualifications of potential appointees;
- heightened attention to the integrity and freedom from conflict of interest of appointees;
- recognition of the need to develop an independent recruiting capability that permits an administration to draw on a number of talent sources in filling appointive positions; and
- preelection planning for the appointment responsibilities of the transition.

This is progress, substantial progress. But in noting that, we need also note that these are only first steps along the path toward a truly effective appointment process capable of serving presidential and national needs into the next century. In the past twenty-five years we have discovered the art of presidential personnel selection. We have not yet perfected it. There are still too many aspects of the appointment process that are not well performed.

The need for an outreach capability has been recognized but not yet adequately implemented. Even in recent years, every administration has drawn its appointees from talent pools much more limited than they need to be.

We have not begun to address effectively the crippling problem of rapid turnover in administrative appointments. To improve consistency in administration and continuity in policy development, much needs to be done to inspire longer job tenure for presidential appointees. An important side effect of this would be a reduction in the recruiting burden as fewer vacancies occurred during the course of an administration.

Though several administrations have begun efforts in this direction, none has yet been very successful in developing procedures for effectively evaluating the on-the-job performance of its appointees. With high turnover, this is critically important. One of the best ways to fill important positions that open up later in an administration is to promote people from subordinate positions who have proven their abilities under fire. That is difficult to do, however, without some reliable system for evaluating personnel, a system that permits those who have performed well to be distinguished from those who have not. To date, inadequate progress has been made in developing such a system.

One of the persistent flaws in the contemporary appointment process is the lack of continuity from one administration to the next. There is no reason to reinvent the wheel every time a new American president is elected. Yet that is precisely what happens. One administration moves out, another moves in; they barely speak to each other in passing. Assistance offered by the old administration is often disdained by the new—part of the latter's insistence on "doing things its own way." The result is that incoming administrations typically find themselves with little upon which to build a sophisticated personnel selection process: no description of appointive positions, no standardized forms for handling paperwork, no guides on valuable sources of talent, no one with experience in the management of the appointment process in the old administration. The errors that occur when any new process is put in operation are repeated in the appointment process at the beginning of almost every administration. They are costly errors because they slow the staffing of the administration and undermine the quality of judgment that is exercised in the selection of appointees.

Finally, it still remains to be seen whether future presidents will recognize the importance of their personal participation in the appointment process. The record to date inspires little optimism in this. A few presidents have taken an active interest in personnel matters: Johnson and Ford most notably. Their interest has proven beneficial to the recruiting and appointment efforts of their administrations. Other presidents, like Eisenhower, Kennedy, and Carter, have been largely indifferent to the appointment process. One, Richard Nixon, came very close to isolating himself from personnel decisions entirely.

One of the important lessons of recent history seems to be that presidential involvement makes a difference in the operations of the appointment process. If a president truly wants to use his appointment powers to enhance his impact on the administrative process, then he is well served by taking a direct part in important personnel matters. Without his participation in decisionmaking and without his active support of their efforts in his behalf, the White House personnel staff will be ill equipped to staff the administration with people who share the president's views and who are fully committed to their implementation.

The appointment process has moved through one important phase in its development and must now begin to move on to the next. Almost three decades of practice and experimentation have generated considerable consensus—over time and across partisan lines—on what the elements of a presidential appointment process ought to be. The need now is to refine each of those elements, to remedy the flaws that linger in the process, and to address squarely those impediments to presidential recruiting that are likely to recur in the years ahead.

NOTES

1. The source of much of the information in this chapter is G. Calvin Mackenzie's comprehensive study of the appointment process, *The Politics of Presidential Appointments* (New York: Free Press, 1981). Those who wish more detail on the history of the appointment process are advised to consult this book.

2. Dwight D. Eisenhower, *Mandate for Change* (New York: Signet Edition, 1963), p. 124.
3. For an incisive discussion of the administrative uses of presidential appointments, see Richard Nathan, *The Administrative Presidency* (New York: Wiley, 1983).

Chapter 3

HOW APPOINTMENTS ARE MADE
Steps in the Process

When one of our earliest presidents had a position to fill in his administration, he would usually decide on his own which of his friends he wanted to fill it. He would call in that person, solicit his services, and then send his name to the Senate, where brief discussion and a perfunctory floor vote would provide confirmation. The president's decision on whom to select, the appointee's decision on whether to accept, and the Senate's decision on confirmation were simple matters that interfered little with the routine administration of the government.

Times have changed. The contemporary appointment process is no longer simple. It has become elaborate and now very much resembles an obstacle course. Appointments, even to positions at low levels in the administrative hierarchy, must now endure a set of routines that are complicated and time consuming. The business of government is often interrupted by delays and dislocations resulting from the normal operations of the appointment process.

In this chapter we will describe the functions that make up the modern appointment process. In so doing, we will attempt to indicate the purpose of each of those functions, the difficulties encountered in their exercise, and the undesirable side effects they sometimes generate. Later in this volume we will explore some ways in which each of these functions might be better performed. Here, however, our purpose is primarily descriptive.

COMPONENTS OF THE PROCESS

Initial Description of Positions

Selection of appointees must begin with some notion of what they are being selected for. Obviously, the clearer that notion, the more likely it is that the chosen candidate will fit the requirements of the job. The appointment process usually starts, therefore, with an attempt by the White House personnel staff to draw an accurate portrait of the nature and needs of the position for which they will be recruiting.

But how is this to be done? Even those personnel staff members who have much government experience are likely to be directly familiar with only a small percentage of the positions a president has to fill. There is much they do not know and most of the time they have no choice but to do some research to fill in the gaps in their own knowledge and sharpen their sensitivity to particular job requirements.

Documents provide them with one source of information. New administrations, especially, find themselves relying on documentary sources because of their basic need to identify the positions for which the president has appointive responsibility. In the last two decades the handbook of the appointment process has been a document produced by the congressional Post Office and Civil Service Committees entitled *Policy and Supporting Positions.* More often it is referred to as the "plum book." It is simply a list of all the non-career positions—political plums—in the federal government. It indicates the location of the job, the name of the incumbent, the appointing authority, the salary, and the expiration date if it has a fixed term. In the past two decades, the plum book has been published every four years at times that coincide with presidential elections.

But the plum book is only a starting point. It does not always distinguish clearly between career and "excepted" positions. It lists appointive positions but provides no information on the kind of work they involve or the kinds of demands their incumbents will have to satisfy. For indications of that, the personnel staff must look elsewhere.

One of the places they typically look is in the statutes that established those positions or that have subsequently amended their jurisdictions. Here they find a formal statement of the location of the job in the administrative hierarchy and an outline of its duties. But even this is rarely enough to satisfy the information needs of the personnel staff. The plum book and the statutes cannot begin to capture the dynamic quality of high-level government positions. Though the description does not change over time, the character of the job may change as new issues come to public prominence, presidential priorities are rearranged, turnover occurs in the composition of congressional committees, and so on. John Macy, who headed Lyndon Johnson's personnel staff, described the problem this way:

> If there was a vacancy as assistant secretary of commerce it wasn't enough to see whether there was some kind of statutory prescription for that particular job. It was a matter of having that and then looking at the job in the context of that particular department at that particular time. What did the chemistry need to be with the secretary? What was important in that particular position? Was it effectiveness in dealing with Congress on legislation? Was it effectiveness in answering interrogation about a particular problem that has come up? Was it a matter of gaining support among interest groups? Was it the need for a high degree of professional specialization in a particular field? Was it need for someone who had a strong administrative background?[1]

Because so many of these questions require current answers, the personnel staff often finds it has no choice but to interview people in the relevant agency, in Congress, in the White House, and sometimes even from outside of government—people who know the position and who can provide a collective sense of what kind of person will be required to handle a particular job well in the two or three years that lie ahead. Together with the documentary sources cited above and the personal knowledge of staff members, these interviews provide the basis from which most job descriptions are drawn.

Over the course of its time in office, each administration develops its own procedures for profiling the positions it has to fill. Its most serious problems with this are usually encountered during the transition. That is when the need for information is most acute because there are so many positions to fill in so short a time. But that is also when it is most difficult to get the kind of current information that is most critical to a successful selection effort. Good sources of that information are not likely yet to have been identified or their reliability tested. The desire to tie informal job requirements to the priorities and administrative approach of the administration will also be impeded because the search for personnel usually begins before these priorities and that approach have been fully defined. Because it is often not clear what role a new administration will prescribe for a particular appointee, it should not be surprising that the fit between job and jobholder sometimes turns out to be less than perfect. That is one of the real perils of the transition period.

Identification of Candidates

The recruiting process begins with the identification of candidates for the vacant position. Finding people who would like the job is no problem; finding people who are well qualified for it is something rather different. There is never a shortage of people willing to accept presidential appointments. There is always a shortage of available people with the talents and experience necessary to do those jobs well. Hence, the problem of identifying candidates is two sided. On the one hand, the personnel staff has to respond to a flood of applications for every job that becomes vacant. On the other, it must undertake a broad search—usually well beyond the group of applications it receives unsolicited—for the best person it can find to fill the job.

The first problem is most cumbersome during the transition, especially if the election brought about a change in party control of the White House. Before the final votes have even been tabulated, résumés, patronage requests, and personnel recommendations begin to flood into transition headquarters—often in recent administrations at the rate of 1,500 a day. Like the sorcerer's apprentice, the personnel staff has to handle the flood control work, even though it is always understaffed and ill prepared for the magnitude of the task.

The problem here is more than just numbers. Many of these unsolicited applications and recommendations will come from people who are politically important to the administration. A courteous and prompt response is necessary to help the president's efforts to build a governing coalition. Many of the applications will also come from people who worked hard for the president's electoral victory, and special care must be taken not to offend that group of strong supporters. So the need to respond to this tidal wave of unsolicited job requests is at once a formidable logistical problem and a matter of great political delicacy.

The historical experience has been, however, that these applications that come in unsolicited rarely provide a new president with the range of talent and depth of experience that many appointive positions require. As one White House personnel aide noted: "Typically, the kind of person we want is not looking for a government job. He's happy where he is, doing something constructive, making more money than we can offer him and has great advancement potential."[2]

One of the lessons from recent history is that searches are usually conducted more thoroughly by the White House than by the individual departments. When the departments conduct the searches, the quality of their candidate identification procedures will vary widely. Some departments will do their jobs well; others will not. When the selection process is centralized in the White House, however, the search for candidates is likely to be more consistent and more thorough. A White House search usually generates a long list of names from a variety of sources. In most cases the nominee is selected from this list.

Evaluation of Candidates

The first shortening of the list of candidates occurs when the personnel staff begins to check references. Inevitably, some candidates will be eliminated at this stage because of questions that occur about their appropriateness for the position under consideration. Political background checks will eliminate some others: those who once worked for an important senator's opponent, for instance, or those who have advocated public policies with which the president disagrees. Further weeding takes place when the personnel staff begins to evaluate the candidates against its own appointment criteria.

Every administration develops some kind of criteria, though some are more explicit than others in specifying them. As a rule, the criteria tend to be general guidelines or talking points that are used to judge the ability of a candidate to fit the management approach and to abide by the policy priorities of an administration. The Kennedy personnel staff, for instance, had a short list of questions it used in evaluating candidates for appointments. It usually included six categories in which the personnel staff was asked to solicit assessments from its references: judgment, toughness, integrity, ability to work with others, industry, and devotion to the principles of the president. The Reagan administration employed a similar set of general appointment criteria: support for Reagan's objectives, integrity, competence, teamwork, toughness, and a commitment to change.

In addition to these general criteria, most personnel searches also employ criteria related to the position under consideration: How well will these people get along with those currently in the agency? Will they be able to manage the budget cuts that the administration intends to implement in that agency? Can they deal effectively with the strong interest group leaders who will try to influence their judgment?

These preliminary evaluations typically occur prior to any direct contact between the White House and the candidates being considered. This is still very much an elimination process in which the principal objective is to reduce a long list of potential candidates down to a short list of well-qualified prospects.

What happens next depends entirely on the selection procedures employed by individual administrations. Three steps remain before the selection process is complete, but different administrations order them in different ways. One is the designation of a primary candidate, another is the conduct of a series of clearances to determine that candidate's acceptability for appointment, and the third is the final selection and recruitment of that candidate. We will examine these steps in this order, but with the cautionary note that the sequence of their implementation is not consistent across administrations or, for that matter, within any single administration.

Designating a Primary Candidate

The selection of a primary candidate from the list of names generated in the search is usually the result of a negotiation process involving the personnel staff, the relevant department or agency, and sometimes the president himself. The critical variable in determining who normally dominates these negotiations is a decision that is likely to have been made by the president early in his administration. It may have been made implicitly or explicitly. It may be a clear decision or a confusing one. It involves the role that department secretaries and agency heads will be permitted to play in the selection process.

If the president has decided to grant a large role to his chief administrative officers in selecting their own subordinates, the designation of a primary candidate will usually be dominated by them. The White House personnel staff may well work with the departments in the search process and even try to influence the choice of a primary candidate. But the upper hand will be held by the department secretaries and agency heads based on their grant of autonomy from the president. Unless it can find good reasons why the candidate is unacceptable, the personnel staff will have little choice but to concur in the designation made by the department.

If the president has chosen, however, to maintain centralized control of the appointment process in the White House, then selection decisions will proceed quite differently. In this case, the White House will be the initiator. While it will work with the appropriate departments in finding mutually satisfactory appointees, these will clearly be presidential selections, with most candidates identified by the White House and the final selection decision controlled there.

We need to be careful not to overstate the predominance of these patterns. Selection decisions are enigmatic. Each is a little drama of its own, and consistency is rare. While tendencies emerge in almost every administration with regard to the allocation of control between the White House and the departments, the fact is that no two decisions are ever made in exactly the same way. Designation of a primary candidate is a critical step in the selection process. The White House and the departments are natural and inevitable competitors for control of it. Each will win some and lose some.

Clearance and Investigation

It is usually after a primary candidate has been designated that the candidate is first informed that he or she is under active consideration for a presidential appointment. The purpose of this is twofold. First, the administration needs to know if the candidate is interested in a presidential appointment and what the likelihood of acceptance is if one is offered. Discussion on this matter is usually delicate because the White House is not yet ready to make that offer. It is simply interested in feeling out the candidate's interest. There is no reason to continue with investigations of a particular person if there is little likelihood that he or she will accept an appointment.

The second reason for contacting candidates at this point is to secure their approval for the background checks that the White House wants to run on them. This is a matter both of simple decency and of respect for a private citizen's right to privacy. The White House will want to initiate an FBI check and, later, other investigations into the candidate's personal history. To do so without informing the candidate is to invite the possibility of embarrassing a person who may never have sought a job in the administration.

The clearance process normally proceeds on several fronts simultaneously. A series of what might be called policy clearances are conducted within the administration to determine that the candidate will be able to support the president's position on the issues that will fall within the jurisdiction of his or her job. The candidate is asked to provide copies of published work and public statements that indicate his or her views on potentially controversial national issues. These and other materials are reviewed by members of the White House staff and appropriate departmental officials to ensure that the candidate's views do not run against the grain of the administration's policies and philosophies.

At the same time, political clearances are being conducted by the White House political affairs staff and the congressional liaison office. The principal purpose of these is to prevent political embarrassment for the administration. Candidates, to be acceptable, must be in good standing with the leadership of the president's party in their home state. There must be no evidence that they have "enemies" on Capitol Hill who might use their appointment as the basis for a confrontation with the administration. And there should be an indication from the Senate committee with confirmation jurisdiction that confirmation is probable.

Another set of clearances is conducted by the Office of the White House Counsel. At this stage in the selection process, the emphasis is on what is called the FBI "name check." This is little more than a computer search of law enforcement files to discover whether the candidate has ever been in any trouble with the law.

The information derived from all of these clearances is usually gathered by the personnel staff and then reviewed and digested. If nothing harmful to the candidate shows up in the clearance process, the nomination will normally proceed to higher levels in the White House, where a decision will be made to nominate the candidate.

The character of this decision varies from one administration to the next. Some presidents choose to take an active part in reviewing and approving candidates recommended by the personnel staff or the departments. Ford, for instance, had frequent contact with his personnel staff, often wanting to hear information about several finalists for each position so that he could make the selection himself. Lyndon Johnson was the most active at this. His night reading often included information on personnel, usually in the form of a several-page memorandum on each important appointment, prepared for him by the personnel staff. The memorandum would include detailed information about the position, a list and description of the top candidates, an assessment of the strengths and weaknesses of each candidate, and a ballot on which Johnson could either make his decision, reject all of the candidates, or ask for more information. Typically, Johnson would return the memorandum to the personnel staff the following morning with his preference indicated.

Other presidents prefer a less active role, however, often simply approving personnel choices that have been made by senior members of the White House staff. For most appointments in the Eisenhower administration, for example, Sherman Adams was the final point of clearance. H. R. Haldeman played a similar role for much of his tenure in the Nixon administration. The character of this final decision is determined almost entirely by the preferences of each president. No role can be formally imposed on a president; each will choose a personnel selection style with which he is most comfortable.

Recruitment and Formal Clearance

Sometimes, recruiting presidential appointees is easy. It is never very difficult, for instance, to find people who are willing to accept a position in the president's cabinet. Those are prestigious offices, fertile with opportunities to affect public policy. They sell themselves. It is also relatively easy to recruit at the outset of a new administration when there is a change in party control of the White House. There will be many talented people anxious to join the new president in correcting what they perceive to be the errors of the previous administration.

But recruiting is not always this easy. Often, in fact, it is one of the most onerous of the burdens of personnel selection. And one of the principal tasks of the White House personnel office is to entice people to join an administration once it has decided whom it wants.

Recruiting is not so much a finite step in the selection process as it is a continuing form of communication between the personnel office and the candidate. Early efforts to elicit candidate interest in the position under consideration usually begin with the first contact. Discussion of the position often continues during the time the candidate's credentials are being reviewed in the clearance processes described above. Finally, when the decision has been made to go ahead with appointment, the administration turns out an aggressive effort to bring the desired candidate on board.

The impediments with which they must deal are well known to White House recruiters. A common one is candidates' concerns about finances. Not everyone loses money in coming to work for the government, but a good many people do, especially those who come from corporations and from major law firms.

Yet another frequently cited reason for which appointment offers are turned down are "personal problems." This is an all-purpose category that covers a variety of concerns. Offers of appointment are refused because candidates fear the impact that long Washington workdays might have on their marriages, or because a child suffers from a disease that requires expensive care, or because an alcohol problem has just been brought under control but might not remain that way in the pressure cooker of political conflict, or because a spouse's career can neither be moved to Washington nor abandoned. These are real and legitimate problems. They are not uncommon. And they are among the most serious impediments the White House confronts in trying to get its appointment offers accepted by the people it wants.

To overcome these impediments, the personnel staff has some enticements it can use. It puts heavy emphasis on trying to sell the candidate on the job, providing information about it and identifying the opportunities it provides for meaningful and creative public service. As a former personnel staff director has noted, "it was imperative to capture the candidate's interest by selling the challenges of the post in question, the broad responsibilities, the opportunity to grow, the President's possible need of his service, and the like."[3] In many ways the uniqueness of these positions is their biggest source of appeal, and White House recruiting efforts are heavily based on that.

Sometimes, recruiters also find it useful to emphasize the patriotic character of public service. This is especially so when they are asking a candidate to take a position that pays considerably less than the one presently held. Gerald Ford's personnel staff found this a particularly important part of their recruiting effort. Faced with the difficulty of attracting people into the government with the dust of Watergate still settling, they tried to indicate to candidates they were pursuing that there had rarely been a time in our history when it was more important for people of talent and integrity to serve their country. It was an approach that the Ford personnel staff found to work remarkably well.

When all else seems to be failing, the biggest gun in the personnel staff's arsenal is the president himself. When a candidate is wavering or uncertain, the offer of an appointment coming directly from the president often has a potent enough impact to ensure acceptance. For a variety of reasons that speak to the respect attaching to his office, most Americans find it hard to turn down a direct request from the president to join his administration. That fact is not lost on the personnel staff which, when it thinks it necessary, will try to take advantage of the clout the president can bring to the recruiting process.

The acceptance of an appointment offer sets in motion the final activities that precede the public announcement of the nomination. These include the FBI "full field investigation" and the formal conflict of interest clearances.

The FBI investigation is left until the end of the selection process because it is time consuming and costly. The investigation usually takes at least two weeks and sometimes as many as eight weeks to complete and costs several thousand dollars. Such investigations have been conducted on presidential appointees since President Eisenhower issued an executive order requiring them in 1953. Eisenhower's principal concern was to determine that his appointees were not security risks. That, however, is only one of the topics covered in the full field investigation.

Once an investigation is ordered by the White House, FBI agents fan out across the country to interview acquaintances of the candidate. These include friends, neighbors, former teachers, and business associates. The FBI's *Manual of Instructions* requires agents to inquire into matters involving "birth, naturalization, education, marital status, employment, military service, relatives, neighbors, associates, references, affiliations with 'questionable organizations,' association with 'questionable individuals,' and taxes."[4] Since 1961, the FBI full field investigation has also included a check with the Internal Revenue Service to determine if income taxes were filed for the previous three years and if there is any record of unpaid taxes, liens, criminal tax investigations, or civil penalties for fraud or negligence.

In conducting these investigations, FBI agents are not instructed to make judgments on the reliability of their sources, only to record what they are told. This information is then digested at FBI headquarters and provided to the White House in summary form. During the years that FBI investigations have been carried out on candidates for appointments, the summaries have usually been handled by a lawyer on the White House staff. Since the mid-1970s, this function has become a responsibility of the White House counsel. While earlier personnel staff directors had often seen the FBI summaries, that has not been the standard operating procedure in recent administrations. Instead, they are examined by the counsel, who informs the personnel staff if the investigation has uncovered information that might jeopardize the appointment.

Over the years, there has been a good deal of criticism of the kind of information that these investigations turn up. One personnel staff director referred to it as a "disjointed, irrelevant collection of gossip." Another said the summaries were like "Fibber McGee's closet—stuff just tumbles out." John Ehrlichman has indicated that he spent his first year at the White House "reading that sort of nonsense" and that he thought the FBI summaries were "very poor jobs, second rate efforts."[5]

Most presidential personnel advisers agree that the FBI investigation rarely sidetracks a nomination. They say it simply doesn't provide them with much reliable information about candidates' abilities, nor does it often generate harmful information about their backgrounds. In fact, in several recent cases where information came to light after the announcement of a nomination, causing withdrawal of that nomination or serious problems for it in the Senate, no warning signals had turned up in the FBI investigation.

The full field investigation does serve a symbolic purpose for the White House and it does protect it from charges that it has been too casual in checking into the backgrounds of its appointees. But it is the almost unanimous testimony of those who are most familiar with the products of these investigations that their practical utility in the appointment process justifies neither their cost nor the time they consume.

The conflict of interest check that also occurs at this stage is a more recent development than the FBI investigation. Systematic conflict of interest checks have been conducted with regularity only since 1971. They were begun in response to the embarrassment of the Nixon administration over a nominee whose confirmation snagged on the revelation of information about his business dealings. None of that information was known to the White House before it was revealed in the confirmation hearing. To prevent a recurrence of the haphazard background check that permitted this, the White House established the practice of requiring all subsequent nominees to disclose all of their financial holdings and to complete an extensive personal data statement.

That statement, and those used by all subsequent administrations, have taken the form of a questionnaire administered by the White House Counsel's office. All nominees have been required to fill out the questionnaire as a condition of appointment. The questions demand an abundance of information and cover several broad areas;

- Financial affairs: employment history, personal and family financial holdings, debts outstanding, current and future employee fringe benefits, and existing contractual obligations
- Legal difficulties: violations of criminal statutes, involvement in criminal investigations, tax law violations, involvement in civil litigation, breaches of ethics or standards of professional conduct
- Involvement in public affairs: participation in elective politics, membership in political organizations, public advocacy of positions on controversial issues
- Areas of potential embarrassment: present or former activities or associations that might be used to embarrass the administration or to impede confirmation

This is a very thorough questionnaire. If completed by candidates in good faith and with candor, it should minimize the likelihood of unpleasant surprises in the confirmation processes or during the appointee's tenure in office.

Since the enactment of the Ethics in Government Act of 1978, a new step has been added to this final set of clearances. That is a conflict of interest examination conducted by the Office of Government Ethics (OGE). OGE is a small agency that has primary responsibility for certifying that nominees are in compliance with existing statutes regulating financial conflicts of interest and other ethical issues. Once the financial disclosure forms have been completed by the nominee, they are sent to the agency in which he will serve. There they are reviewed, usually by the agency's ethics counselor, and an opinion is provided on the extent to which the nominee's personal finances pose a potential conflict of interest with the responsibilities he will encounter in office. That opinion is forwarded to OGE. If a problem has arisen, an effort is made by OGE to find a cure before the nomination is reviewed by the Senate. When that has been accomplished, the OGE director writes to the chairman of the appropriate Senate committee indicating that the nominee "is in compliance with applicable laws and regulations concerning conflicts of interest."

The FBI full field investigation, the completion of the personal data statement, and assurance of compliance with conflict of interest regulations mark the final steps in the selection process. When all of these are completed, assuming that no insurmountable problems have arisen, the nomination goes forward to the Senate.

Senate Confirmation

The confirmation process usually involves three stages: prehearing information gathering by the appropriate committee, the hearing itself, and a vote by the full Senate. During the prehearing period, which typically lasts two or three weeks between the announcement of the nomination and the start of the hearing, several kinds of information are provided to the committee. It receives a financial disclosure statement from the nominee and the OGE director's letter reporting on any potential conflicts of interest. Some committees also ask nominees to provide other kinds of information, including answers to questions about substantive issues they will deal with in their new jobs. There is, however, little consistency in the kinds of information that individual committees seek or in the formats in which they choose to have it presented.

If any information appears at this stage that raises questions in the minds of committee members about the qualifications of the nominee, the hearing may be postponed until a committee investigation is undertaken and completed. This is most likely to occur if opposition to the nomination has arisen after its announcement and charges have been made against the nominee that require further examination. Investigations of this sort are rare but not unknown.

This is also a time when the nominee is preparing for the confirmation hearing. Few patterns prevail in the way this preparation is carried out. Some nominees make an effort to visit individually with the members of the committee that will oversee their confirmation. Others do not. Some senators expect this as a matter of course. Others find it a time-consuming burden and prefer to put off their first meeting with the nominee until the hearing itself.

The way in which nominees prepare themselves for the questioning they will encounter at confirmation hearings is highly variable. A nominee to a major position like a cabinet post, especially one who will have to confront a series of difficult issues soon after taking office, is likely to be assisted in his preparations for confirmation by the White House and by personnel from the department to which he has been nominated. This preparation might involve extensive briefings, clear instructions on the president's policy views in this area, and even some rehearsal of answers for questions that are likely to be asked at the hearing.

Preparation to this extent is unusual, however. Many nominees, especially those to positions below cabinet level, are offered little assistance by the White House or by the organization in which their new job is located. They are forced to prepare by themselves and often do so inadequately. In part, this is a result of the absence in most administrations of anyone in the White House who is assigned responsibility for assisting nominees after they have accepted the president's job offer. The personnel staff often believes its work is done when that acceptance is received. It goes on to other things, leaving new nominees to fend for themselves.

This is also a time when the nominee is consumed with the details of terminating current employment, righting financial affairs, and moving to Washington. Even if more abundant opportunities for substantive preparation were available, there would be little time to fit them in. The result of all of this is that nominees often approach their confirmation hearing with little confidence in their ability to handle the questions that may be asked of them.

The character of confirmation hearings defies simple generalization. Each committee has its own quirks and traditions and each senator his or her own definition of how the confirmation process ought to be conducted. Many senators believe their responsibility is only to ensure that a nominee satisfies the minimum standards of competence and integrity. Others, however, believe it their duty to determine that nominees meet the highest standards of competence, integrity, and expertise. The character of the confirmation hearing will largely depend on which kind of senator serves as committee chair.

Most confirmation hearings are short, friendly, and perfunctory. The nominee is typically introduced by a senator from his home state and then warmly welcomed by the presiding committee member. General questions are likely to follow about the nominee's financial statement and his or her willingness to consult with the Senate should it seek information in the future. A few broad questions may be asked about the issues that the nominee will have to confront in office, but these questions are rarely penetrating or hostile. Most hearings last half an hour or less and end in a unanimous vote in favor of confirmation.

Though that is the normal procedure, there are enough exceptions to the norm to stir fears of the confirmation hearing in the hearts of many nominees. The hearings that attract the most publicity—and are, therefore, the ones with which nominees are most familiar—are those in which hard questioning and personal attacks take place. Several factors may account for such variations from the norm.

One is the importance of the office under consideration. A nominee to a major cabinet office or to the position of director of the FBI, the Environmental Protection Agency, the Agency for International Development, or the Bureau of Indian Affairs should never expect a pro forma confirmation hearing. The high-profile importance of these positions and the passions generated by the issues with which they deal almost guarantee controversy. Nominees to these posts are natural candidates for close examination and for criticism by those likely to disagree with the policies they will pursue in office.

Other factors may also generate heat at a confirmation hearing. A past indiscretion by the nominee—a tax problem, involvement in a civil suit, or a poor driving record, for instance—is an invitation for an embarrassing line of questioning. Many nominees are public figures whose writings or speeches may include statements that have to be defended or, if they are out of line with the president's program, explained away. The hearing also provides an opportunity for critical testimony from opponents of the nomination. They may oppose it because they have had unpleasant dealings with the nominee in the past and think him or her unfit for public office, or because they disagree with his or her views on an important public issue. Any of these occurrences can contribute mightily to the nominee's discomfort level during the confirmation hearing.

The hearing is usually followed by an executive session of the committee in which there is a vote on confirmation. If the vote is to confirm, then the nomination is reported to the Senate floor. Except in the most controversial cases, or for the most important offices, no written report is prepared on the nomination. In nearly every instance, all that is reported is the commiteee's recommendation on confirmation.

A floor vote usually follows shortly after the committee has concluded its deliberations, often on the same day. Of the hundred or more major nominations that come before the Senate each year, the vast majority are dealt with by voice vote. Recorded votes are taken on only a handful in each session of Congress.

Nearly all nominations are confirmed by the Senate. Those who are not likely to be confirmed have probably been identified in the clearance process by the White House personnel office and their names removed from consideration. Hence, those few nominations that fail are usually the result of information that appears after the announcement that was either unknown to the White House or underestimated in importance. When a nomination is defeated, that defeat almost always occurs in committee. Nominations have been rejected on the Senate floor less than half a dozen times since 1960.

SUMMARY

What we have described here is a complex, multistaged, participatory process. It has been shaped over time to serve a variety of objectives and to satisfy the concerns of a number of interested parties. As an example, Figure 3-1 provides a schema of the sequence of the appointment process in the first year of the Reagan administration.

If the implementation of White House personnel selection procedures were as thorough and effective as the structure of this process intends, the needs of the president for able subordinates and the desire of the public for competent and honest leaders would be well served, with few exceptions. Implementation often falls short of those standards, however.

- Job descriptions have not always been developed with the clarity and sophistication necessary to permit reliable identification of appropriately qualified candidates.
- Candidate searches are too often truncated and narrowly focused, failing to identify or explore fertile sources of talent across the country.
- Assessments of candidates for appointment are sometimes undertaken hurriedly, leaving little time for careful analysis or comparison of each individual's qualifications for the specific position under consideration. At other times, the evaluation and clearance

Figure 3-1. Reagan Appointments Clearance Process, July 1981.

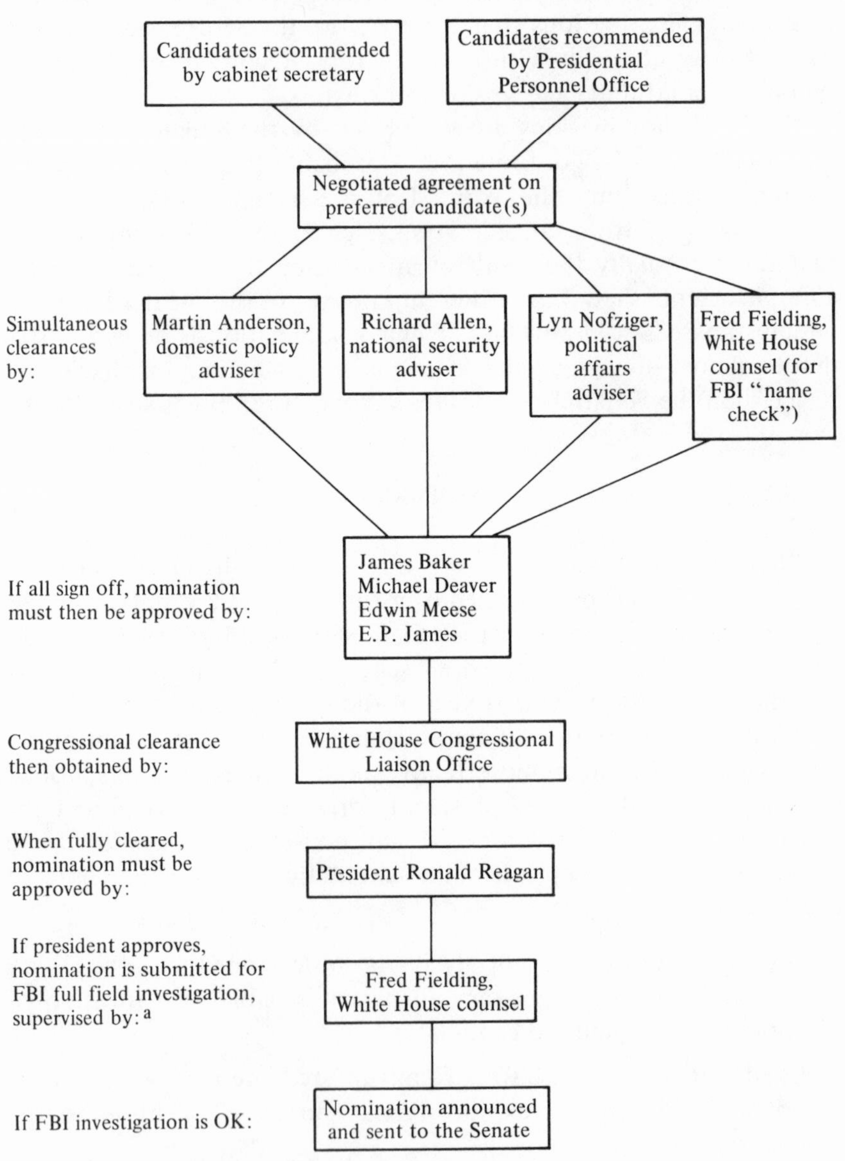

a. Simultaneously, the Office of Government Ethics informally reviews financial disclosure statements with the White House counsel. Usually, fifteen days before the nomination goes to Senate, OGE formally reviews and begins preparation of the report to the Senate committee.

Source: *Government Service: A Proposal for Action*, Report of the Business Roundtable, October 20, 1981, p. 9.

process drags on for so long that appointments are delayed and the efficient conduct of the business of government is interrupted.

- Recruitment efforts may fail to overcome the doubts of those who are reluctant to leave the security and financial prosperity of their current position for the challenging but uncertain opportunities provided by a presidential appointment. This has been a special problem in those administrations where the president was not actively involved in personnel selection and was thus unwilling to serve as a recruiter for his own administration.
- Background investigations of designated candidates have rarely been a source of satisfaction to the White House or of comfort to the candidate. The FBI's full field investigation produces gossip, speculation, and a variety of unverified opinions but little hard information on the talents or personality traits of the people being investigated.
- The financial disclosure and conflict of interest checks, now much more systematically organized and carefully implemented by the White House counsel and the OGE, remain a deep and often disagreeable intrusion on the private financial affairs of candidates for appointment. The unpleasantness and the financial sacrifices required by compliance are sometimes sufficient to deter highly qualified candidates from accepting an invitation to join a presidential administration.
- Those who do accept too frequently find that they are left on their own to move their families to Washington, to prepare for confirmation hearings, to familiarize themselves with the political realities of working in the capital city, and to acquire substantive information about their new jobs. At a time when it is most needed, staff and other kinds of support for new appointees is hardest to come by.
- The confirmation process, though an important constitutional check on the quality of appointments, is fraught with further opportunities for humiliation of nominees and for delay in the appointment process. Because of diversity in the operating styles of individual committees, preparation for confirmation adds yet another layer of complexity to an appointment process that is plenty complicated already.

The appointment process that has been put in place over the past several decades is sound in many ways. In others, however, it is inadequate—or at least it has been employed with inadequate diligence, consistency, and political sensitivity. To improve the quality of presidential appointees two paths must be pursued simultaneously. One requires a shoring up of those aspects of the appointment process that have not served the objectives of that process as well as they might. This may require structural and procedural changes instituted by the White House, by some agencies and departments, by the FBI, and by the Senate. In one or two instances, changes may also be required in the laws that regulate presidential appointments.

But even that may not be enough to ensure the wise operation of the appointment process. Procedure is only one part of that; human judgment is another. Sound procedures can abet, but cannot substitute for, good judgment by those who make appointment decisions. The second requirement for improving the quality of presidential appointees, therefore, is for presidents to select carefully those who participate in the appointment process and to sensitize them to the importance of their task and to the diversity of concerns that should affect their choices.

NOTES

1. Interview of John W. Macy, Jr., conducted by Emmette S. Redford and Richard L. Schott, Washington, D.C., September 11, 1976. Used with permission.
2. Quoted in Dom Bonafede, "Nixon Personal Staff Works to Restructure Federal Policies," *National Journal* 3 (November 12, 1971): 2446.
3. Frederic V. Malek, *Washington's Hidden Tragedy* (New York: Free Press, 1978), p. 72.
4. Federal Bureau of Investigation, *Manual of Instructions*, Sec. 19 (B)(3) (a-y).
5. Each of the statements quoted in this paragraph first appeared in U.S. Senate, Committee on Government Operations, *Study on Federal Regulation: The Regulatory Appointments Process*, 95th Congress, 1st Session, 1977, p. 141.

Chapter 4

THE FEDERAL EXECUTIVE'S WORK ENVIRONMENT
Problems for Recruiting and Retention

The president's success in recruiting the people he wants to serve in his administration and in retaining their services throughout his term is heavily dependent on the satisfaction that his appointees anticipate and experience in the federal work environment. They will be more inclined to accept his offer of appointment if they think that environment is hospitable to the kind of effective service they hope to provide; they will be more inclined to stay if that is in fact what they find on the job. The appeal of the jobs the president has to offer is a central factor in his ability to recruit and retain highly qualified people to fill them.

Much of the evidence we explored in preparing this volume indicated that perceptions of the federal executive work environment inspire a mixture of reactions. In the view of many people who have worked in both the public and the private sector, the excitement and stimulation provided by the former is rarely matched in the latter. For example, James H. Rowe, Jr., who served in the administration of Franklin Roosevelt before pursuing a successful private law practice, noted of his public service: "There are not better jobs in the world. I haven't done anything so important since."[1]

Rowe's is not an uncommon reflection but neither is it a universal one. Nor is it the prevailing perception among those who have never served in the public sector. We have also found in our explorations that many people have left federal service because of frustrations with their jobs, their salaries, or the highly charged environment in which they were forced to operate. We have also found that in many segments of the private sector perceptions of the character of the public service heavily emphasize its negative aspects. Public service is perceived as perilous and frustrating rather than as a source of excitement and opportunity. For many technical specialists and mid-career executives in the private sector, whose managerial skills and technical expertise make them prime candidates for subcabinet positions, public life too often seems forbidding rather than enticing. Instead of challenge they see frustration. Instead of opportunity they see rigidity and complexity. Instead of career enhancement they see career interruption.

Though we recognize the genuine rewards of public service and the intense satisfaction that many people have experienced from it, we want to concentrate in this chapter on what we believe is a growing negative perception of the character of the environment in which presidential appointees work—a perception that has substantial consequences in terms of the president's recruiting efforts. We will focus especially on the substance of those perceptions and on some of the reasons they have continued to prevail.

LIFE IN THE PUBLIC EYE

The Media and the Fishbowl

Even the most visible executives from the private sector rarely are prepared for the public exposure that normally accompanies government service. Washington is a reporter's paradise—one of the most important news centers of the world. In addition to the elite press corps familiar to readers of national newspapers or viewers of network television, there are thousands of other reporters who work for regional news organizations, small-city dailies, and the trade press. With so many reporters at work in one place, there is little that happens in Washington that doesn't somehow qualify as newsworthy. For those who work as presidential appointees, that means that the glare of public attention rarely dims. Any action or decision of a public executive is likely to be a matter of interest to some segment of the news media. Public life comes to mean just that: life in public.

In a democracy, of course, there is much to admire in this. A free press is an important bulwark of freedom and fairness. The knowledge that a public official's actions are closely watched and likely to be reported ought to serve as a disincentive to injustice, malfeasance, and corruption. The free press is an important instrument of accountability. Few would deny any of this.

But in the environment of contemporary Washington, where competition in the news business is intense and aggressive, reporters and editors are often drawn to report more than just the formal actions and decisions of political executives. Instead, they often seek to identify the motives of the decisionmakers, the disagreements that occur among them, and the inadequacies of the decisions they make. In the intensity of this journalistic competition, attention often comes to focus on the trivial, the personal, and the negative.

The news that journalists believe most likely to sell newspapers and attract viewers is often not the news that federal executives enjoy reading or seeing. Reporting in Washington often emphasizes personality over policy, conflict over consensus, strategy over substance, and error over achievement. This kind of reporting tends to polarize and exacerbate conflict on issues. It often also undermines authority and contributes to the difficulty in resolving public problems.

In this kind of environment, government officials who might want to test new approaches in a search for consensus often hold back for fear of having their ideas pounced upon and repudiated or belittled. For every idea that emanates from a government executive the press is able to find a critic—too often, with little regard for the critic's credentials or understanding of the complexities of the problem. John G. Kemeny, a university president who headed the presidential commission that studied the Three Mile Island nuclear accident, noted his concern at this phenomenon by indicating that he someday expected to read the following story: "Three scientists by the names of Galileo, Newton, and Einstein have concluded that the earth is round. However, the *New York Times* has learned authoritatively that Professor John Doe has conclusive evidence that the earth is flat."[2]

Nothing is more likely to generate media interest than an indiscretion committed by a public servant, even if the commission was inadvertent. The past decade has provided us with enough examples of this to permit a composite sketch of the scenario that usually unfolds when such an indiscretion occurs. The affected public official suddenly finds that his or her every step is followed by a pack of reporters. The hallway outside that official's office will become a stakeout for reporters and photographers; so too will the front lawn of the official's house. Pictures will be taken and questions shouted whenever the official appears in public. Congressmen, eager to get into the act, will call the official to testify on the matters in question. The president will be pressured to declare his confidence in the official or to ask for a resignation. As the atmosphere heats up, it becomes difficult for the affected public official to clear up the matter. The work of the agency is impeded, and public confidence in both the official and the agency appears to weaken.

While events of this sort are hardly commonplace in Washington, they have occurred often enough to worry even the most confident and experienced government executives. By focusing on mistakes, often without due regard to their magnitude or motive, the news media inspire excessive caution on the part of public officials. This, in turn, forces those officials to spend significant amounts of time on trivial matters, employing whatever caution is necessary to avoid making a mistake—no matter how small—that might become a focus of media attention. Frank C. Carlucci, one of our most experienced public servants, recently noted that it is "becoming much more difficult to accomplish a mission in government" because of the premium we put on "over-the-shoulder watchers."[3]

The news media's preoccupation with personalities, rumor, and gossip has blurred the distinction between news and entertainment. In so doing, it has begun to erase the line between the public responsibilities and private lives of government officials. Reporter and media critic Sander Vanocur has been a leader in questioning these tendencies in the media. "Under the title, 'The People's Right to Know'," he has said, "they practice journalism's right to titillate."[4]

By focusing on controversy and failure, the press fuels public cynicism. The aberrations reported by the news media become the norm in the public mind, and this becomes a bssis for perceptions—misleading as they are—of public service and public servants. In addition to weakening public confidence in government, the effect of this is to repel a number of potential presidential appointees who do not want to put their career opportunities and their good reputations in jeopardy at the hands of the aggressive community of Washington journalists.

Time Demands and Family Life

It is hard work being a federal political executive. Because of their technical, social, and political complexity, public problems defy simple solutions. Decisionmaking itself is enormously complicated. The reasons are many: the contemporary diffusion of political authority, the growth of executive and congressional staffs, the increase in the number of organized special interests, and the difficulty in confining problems to narrow institutional jurisdictions, to name a few. No significant decision can be made without wide and careful consultation. Even that may not produce consensus sufficient to resolve a problem, thus stretching out the decisionmaking process.

Time is an invaluable asset for a political executive, but there is rarely enough of it available. The time demands on presidential appointees are staggering. Interest group lobbyists, reporters, and other government officials fill their in-boxes with memos and phone messages and their calendars with meetings—some substantive, others ceremonial. Congressional committees call upon them frequently for their testimony. The management needs of their own program or agency constantly require their attention. The annual budget cycle also consumes a good deal of their time.

Short-term problems always seem to take precedence over long-term concerns. Crisis management frequently comes to characterize the day-to-day activities of many presidential appointees. Perspectives are shortened, creativity and imagination are squeezed out, and little time is left for reflection. There are few opportunities to develop bold, long-range approaches to persistent problems.

Further compounding these frustrations is the proliferation of interest groups in American politics. Most federal executives are shadowed by groups with a direct interest in the problems and policies under their jurisdiction. Many of these groups employ skilled lobbyists and talented lawyers. They operate intensive communications networks, and they have their own political action committees contributing money to candidates. They are sophisticated operators in the political arena, and their number and effectiveness have contributed to the growing fragmentation and polarization of contemporary political decisionmaking. Government executives often feel themselves whipsawed by competing groups, each locked into its own fixed point of view. No matter what policy executives decide to pursue, some groups are bound to be angered. In their reactions, the groups do little to make life easier for those executives.

This environment produces several effects, most of them frustrating to public officials. One is that those executives are required to spend long days at the office. Those who escape ten- to twelve-hour days and six- or seven-day weeks are a very small minority of presidential appointees. The barriers this poses to a satisfying family life are obvious. Too many public executives feel that they face the Hobson's choice of leading sane family lives or of being effective public servants and that the two objectives are almost impossible to reconcile.

Another impact of the long hours, often under heavy pressure, is burnout. The average tenure of presidential appointees in a single job is less than two years. Efforts by some administrations to extend that tenure have not been notably successful. There are many reasons for this, one of the most common being, simply, that government executives are worn out by the pace at which they feel compelled to work.

The image of the federal executive as a prizefighter punch drunk from too many battles in the political arena is not an entirely false one. These are very demanding, pressure-laden jobs, and that fact is widely recognized. Those who accept these positions often do not stay in them for very long. Others, recognizing the burdens of public service, choose not to take them at all. Successful presidential recruiting is impeded as a result.

The Negative View of Government

Negative public attitudes toward government have long been a major obstacle to building a strong public service in the United States. Editorial cartoonists and humorists have ridiculed political figures from the earliest days of our nation. As we worked our way out of the depression and through World War II and the Korean War, the level of cynicism decreased and a more positive bond was built between the government and its citizens. But Vietnam, Watergate, and the economic failures of the past two decades have led again to a decline in confidence in government. In reviewing the new realities of public opinion, pollster Daniel Yankelovich has concluded: "Perhaps the sharpest shift in American attitudes has been a steady erosion of trust in government and other institutions, falling from a peak of trust and confidence in the late fifties to a trough of mistrust in the early eighties."[5]

It is no simple matter to track the source of these negative attitudes. Perhaps one of their most significant sources, however, is the paradoxical nature of public expectations. On the one hand, the public expresses little confidence in government. On the other, it expects the government to pursue effectively an extraordinary range of public policies: increase defense spending, reduce taxes, maintain welfare services, and balance the federal budget. When government fails to satisfy these unrealistic demands, public confidence in it wanes and the competence of public servants is called into question.

Unrealistic public demands are often fueled by politicians who promise more than they can deliver. They talk of lofty policy goals, yet at the same time castigate the public service with denunciations of red tape, inefficient bureaucrats, and "puzzle palaces on the Potomac." As government gets more complex, political debate gets more simplistic. Too frequently, the result is that the gap between expectation and performance is widened, making even the best efforts of public executives inadequate to satisfy the expectations placed upon them.

Sources of difficulty in this regard are the campaign statements made by presidential candidates. The last two successful candidates, Jimmy Carter and Ronald Reagan, both carried out withering attacks on the federal bureaucracy during their campaigns, emphasizing all that was negative in public attitudes about government. If that was good politics, it turned out not to be very good management. When those two adminsitrations came to power, each found a declining morale in the career civil service and senior career executives who were naturally wary of those administrations' political appointees and program objectives. Perhaps even more distressing, and ironic, was the difficulty these administrations encountered in recruiting from the private sector—a difficulty exacerbated by the negative view of government that campaign rhetoric had helped to perpetuate.

The prevalence of this negative view of government in the corporate world has sometimes been a serious impediment to presidential recruitment from that source. In part, this is because potential appointees themselves may share those negative attitudes. An equally large problem, however, is the attitude of corporate leaders who are reluctant to encourage their technical people and midcareer managers to enter public service, who see little value in it, and who may even see it as an obstruction to upward mobility within the corporate world. As long as those attitudes prevail among corporation leaders, recruitment from that source will remain a difficult task.

Talented people are not generally drawn to enterprises that are not admired by the public. Negative public attitudes and the actions of the news media, elected officials, and interest groups feed on each other in very destructive ways. The inaccurate stereotypes of the public service make it difficult to recruit and maintain top-flight people. The significance of this problem was captured by Yale University President A. Bartlett Giamatti: "If a society assumes its politicians are venal, stupid or self-serving, it will attract to its public life as an ongoing self-fulfilling prophecy the greedy, the knavish and the dim."[6]

THE TRANSITION FROM PRIVATE TO PUBLIC SECTOR

For those presidential appointees who are not put off by the stereotype of public life described above, there remain a number of genuine and distressing obstacles to effective service as a government executive. These obstacles loom especially large for those coming to government from the private sector and are most acute for those doing so for the first time.

Relocation Costs

Take the case of a typical corporate executive from a midwestern city who has been recruited for a subcabinet position by the president, his first experience in the federal government. Once he has decided to accept the position, his first concern is moving to Washington.

He will immediately find himself confronting two substantial expenses. One is the cost of purchasing or renting a residence in the Washington area; the other is the cost of moving there. Washington remains one of the most expensive housing markets in the country, and it is the rare presidential appointee who doesn't wind up with a larger mortgage or a smaller house when coming to work for the federal government. Since most do not stay very long, there is little time to build equity or to benefit from appreciating home values. Thus, the change of residences is usually a financially costly proposition.

A good many appointees recruited from the private sector are surprised to learn that the federal government has no program for reimbursement for moving expenses. These must be borne entirely by the appointee. If he or she is moving an entire household, as is typically the case, this is no small expense. Before the job has even begun, the government executive coming from the private sector has already made a significant financial sacrifice.

Navigating the Confirmation Process

The next problem that has to be confronted is the confirmation process. This is a prospect that people new to government find particularly fearsome. *Fortune* magazine warned in 1977 that more and more nominees from the private sector have found the confirmation process to be an "excruciating ordeal of self-exposure and public criticism."[7] John Post, the former head of the Washington office of The Business Roundtable, expressed this view: "The whole confirmation process is in many cases a very demeaning process. You have to go up there hat in hand and then you go through a very, very severe examination. We still run into too many cases where good people will not accept even consideration for appointment because of the process they'd have to go through." Some of these fears could be mitigated by a systematic effort by the White House personnel staff to prepare people for their confirmation hearings, but, as stated previously, such preparation is rarely provided.

Fears about the vagaries of the confirmation process are not unjustified. It is true, of course, that the vast majority of presidential nominees are confirmed, usually without controversy or hostility. With the recent growth in Senate committee staff, however, a number of Senate committees now conduct their own investigations of nominees. They often dredge up information that has little relevance to the nomination or the nominee's qualifications for the position under consideration but is potentially embarrassing to the nominee and perhaps even to the administration. The publicity value in that is not lost on staff members looking for ways to attract attention for the senators for whom they work. More than a few recent nominees have found themselves answering questions about a minor run-in with police in their youth, nuisance lawsuits in which they became involved as part of the routine of corporate life, incorrectly quoted or out-of-context statements from old newspaper articles, and the like. Not knowing in advance how or if they are going to be challenged at their confirmation hearings, presidential nominees are plagued by the anxiety of uncertainty. Little is done to mitigate that.

Learning a New Job

In the private sector, one rarely takes over a new position without prior preparation for it. That may be in the nature of formal training—as with engineers, loan officers, or accountants—or it may take the form of a break-in period, during which the person about to assume a position spends some time shadowing the person who currently holds it. In the public sector neither model often obtains. There are few political executive positions for which any formal training programs exist. This would not be so troublesome if opportunities existed for new appointees to go through a break-in period during which they could learn the parameters of their job from their predecessors. But that doesn't often occur either. New appointees usually arrive on the job after their predecessors have left. This is especially true at the outset of a new administration when few remnants of the old team remain to break in the new.

This lack of orientation also complicates the transition of new appointees from the private sector. They must learn their jobs as they do them, and that increases the likelihood of slow starts and mistakes, which may do little to win the respect of the career executives in their agencies and which may even earn them critical public attention. Most conscientious new appointees do eventually master their jobs, but in the time it takes them to do so, important decisions may be delayed or untracked. This little serves the needs of the president or the nation.

Orientation to the Government Environment

An equally important need for those coming into government service for the first time is preparation for the new political environment in which they will operate. Public life is different from private life in such significant ways that the failure of an administration to orient its recruits to their new surroundings is a significant oversight.

There are a number of topics on which new appointees would benefit from the advice of seasoned Washington veterans. Most have never before dealt with the Congress or with any other kind of legislature. They would realize great value from information on how that institution works and guidance on the best ways to develop mutually beneficial relationships with its members. Many new appointees are also inexperienced in dealing with the press. They lack a clear sense of reporting techniques, the way journalists cultivate and use sources, the importance of deadlines, and the jargon of "for attribution," "backgrounders," "deep backgrounders," and so on. They are also unlikely to have much experience before a television camera or a live microphone.

New appointees also have much to learn about interest groups, their objectives, and the techniques they employ to influence public policy. Similarly, they are not likely to have much knowledge or understanding of the career civil service. In fact, quite to the contrary, they may well possess a number of misperceptions about the career service. The establishment of effective working relationships with career employees is especially important for a government executive, and it is an objective that a useful orientation program should certainly pursue.

Public management is another area in which new appointees would benefit from careful preparation. As indicated previously, all of them will encounter enormous demands on their time. If they are prepared for this and advised in ways to respond effectively to those demands, they will be more effective and happier in their jobs. There is in Washington at any given time a community of federal government veterans, wise in the ways of public management, who could impart some of the important lessons of their experience to these new appointees. This would be a considerable service to them.

Some attempts have been made in recent administrations to develop orientation programs of this sort. The Ford administration carried this out with a considerable degree of success and the Reagan administration conducted efforts in this direction as well. But, though widely recognized as a good idea, orientation programs for new appointees have not been widely or consistently implemented.

In this regard, the executive branch of the federal government now lags behind the Congress and the federal judiciary, and behind the state governors as well, in its procedures for orienting new personnel. The Congress has for more than a decade conducted a number of orientation programs, both for new members and for their staffs. New appointees to the federal bench receive a thorough orientation in judicial procedures and administration. The National Governors Association has developed a series of programs designed to prepare newly elected governors for the tasks they will face when they assume office. For new presidential appointees, however, few such opportunities exist.

THE COMPENSATION FACTOR

Determining appropriate levels of compensation for employees is a difficult task for a democratic government. Democratic principles pull in two directions. On the one hand, there is the desire to attract into government service the best people the country has to offer and thus to provide financial incentives powerful enough for that purpose. On the other hand, citizens in a democracy are uncomfortable when their leaders are earning salaries vastly larger than their own. The problem of setting compensation levels is further complicated by our history of treating this as a political decision to be made by the most intensely political of our institutions: the Congress. Much as they may desire to set government salaries high enough to attract talented people into the public service, members of Congress are profoundly sensitive to the electoral backlash that federal pay policies can inspire. For these reasons, the establishment of compensation levels for government executives has always been an extremely painful enterprise.

One important impact of this is that, with few exceptions, executives in the private sector are better paid than those holding positions at similar levels of responsibility in the public sector. The obvious consequence of this disparity is that presidential appointees recruited from the private sector usually have to accept a salary reduction as part of the price of public service.

This suggests that federal executive compensation is probably an impediment to presidential recruiting from the private sector. That appears, in fact, to be the case, though the situation is more complicated than it may seem at first blush. For some categories of executive positions and for some types of appointees, compensation is a relatively minor recruiting impediment. Presidents rarely experience much difficulty, for instance, in recruiting people to serve in their cabinets, even though those who do so often take substantial cuts in pay. It is also relatively easy to recruit Supreme Court justices, ambassadors, and leaders in particularly prominent agencies like the FBI and the Securities and Exchange Commission. Salary concerns are also of little consequence to potential appointees who are young, who have never held a high-salaried position, or who are anxious, for career advancement reasons, to acquire the advantages of government experience. In any administration there will be a number of appointees making more money than they have ever made before.

But the evidence we have gathered from presidential recruiters and from corporate officials indicates clearly that compensation levels are a problem in recruiting technical specialists and midcareer executives from the private sector for subcabinet and agency positions. While these are people whose energy, creativity, and expertise are much needed by the government, they are also the ones for whom the financial demands of government service are most difficult to bear. Many of them are just reaching their peak earning years and have not yet built up the cushion that a large investment portfolio can provide. They usually find themselves paying off large mortgages and trying at the same time to pay tuition costs for their children. To accept a presidential appointment and the income reduction that it requires at such a point in their lives is not an appealing prospect. That explains, in large part, why this group of people is one of the most resistant to the entreaties of presidential recruiters.

Compensation Determination

The current system by which federal executive salaries are determined was established by the Postal Revenue and Federal Salary Act of 1967. Under this act, a nine-member Commission on Executive, Legislative, and Judicial Salaries is established in the last year of each presidential term (hence the familiar name, quadrennial commission or "quad com"). The commission reports to the president, who makes salary recommendations in his annual budget message. Under the 1967 act's provisions, the president's recommendations were to take effect thirty days after their submission to Congress unless either house of Congress disapproved or the Congress enacted an alternative salary structure. This procedure was amended in 1977, however, when the Congress required roll call votes in both houses on pay increases. In 1975, the Executive Salary Cost-of-Living Adjustment Act was enacted to supplement the commission process by providing annual cost-of-living pay adjustments during the period between quadrennial commissions. Annual adjustments for federal executives now equal the average general schedule employee's pay increase under the Federal Pay Comparability Act of 1970.

This history of salary increases for federal executives demonstrates that this process has not succeeded either in keeping public executive compensation from falling further behind the private sector or in maintaining the purchasing power of federal executive salaries. Between 1969 and 1976 federal executives received only one raise—for 5 percent in 1975. In 1972 the appointment of the quadrennial commission was delayed and so too were the president's recommendations. When they were forwarded to the Congress, the Senate rejected them in a lopsided election year vote. In 1977, following the recommendations of the quadrennial commission, the salary of assistant secretaries was increased by just over 25 percent to $50,000. In 1978, however, Congress accepted President Carter's proposal to freeze executive pay. A raise of 5.5 percent was approved in 1979. The 1980 quadrennial commission recommended another substantial raise, but President Reagan's Executive Level I and II appointees did not receive a pay increase until 1983—a result of late 1982 congressional action raising the ceiling.

The results of this unpredictable salary determination mechanism can be clearly seen by examining the salaries of most assistant secretaries (Executive Level IV) and comparing them with increases in the cost of living and in private sector salaries during the past fourteen years. In 1969, the annual salary for assistant secretaries was raised to $38,000. By 1983 it had reached $67,200, an increase of 77 percent since 1969. Cabinet secretaries are paid $80,100, an increase of just 33 percent since 1969. By comparison, the cost of living has risen by more than 150 percent during this period. Data provided to the 1980 quadrennial commission by consultants (Hay Associates) show that those in top management positions in the private sector—chief financial officers, division marketing heads, and division general managers—received salary increases of more than 116 percent between April 1969 and April 1980. Those in middle-management positions—directors of labor relations and plant managers—received salary increases in excess of 120 percent. The commission recommended that salaries of assistant secretaries be increased to $75,000 in 1980. Three years later, in 1983, they still remain below the recommended level.

Table 4-1 indicates the pattern of salary increases over the past fourteen years in each of the executive level pay categories.

One of the principal reasons for the inconsistent pattern of federal executive salary increases is a practice adopted in 1969 of linking the

Table 4-1. Federal Executive Compensation, 1969-83.[a]

Executive Level (with representative positions)	*1969*	*1977*	*1983*	*Percentage Increase 1969-83*	*1980 Commission Recommendation*
I. (cabinet officers)	$60,000 (12)[b]	$66,000 (13)	$80,100 (14)	33.5%	$95,000
II. (deputy secretaries of major departments, heads of major agencies)	42,500 (64)	57,500 (70)	69,800 (66)	64%	85,000
III. (deputy secretaries of minor departments, heads of middle agencies)	40,000 (88)	52,500 (118)	68,400 (129)	71%	80,000
IV. (assistant secretaries, general counsels)	38,000 (261)	50,000 (385)	67,200 (307)[c]	77%	75,000
V. (directors of major units of agencies)	36,000 (240)	47,500 (269)	63,800 (68)[c]	77%	70,000

a. Modest increases went into effect in 1975, 1979, and 1981 (for Levels III-V).
b. Indicates number of positions.
c. Pursuant to the Civil Service Reform Act of 1978, Executive Levels IV and V that do not require Senate confirmation became part of the Senior Executive Service.

salaries of officials in Executive Level II to those of members of Congress. Under this practice, executive salary decisions pivot on congressional salary decisions. And, as indicated above, members of Congress always find it politically difficult to raise their own salaries, especially if an election is approaching. Nothing more clearly reflects this difficulty than the fact that congressional pay has been increased less than a dozen times in this century. As long as the linkage of executive and congressional salaries remains in effect, there appears little likelihood of establishing an executive compensation system that is objective and consistent.

Compensation and the Recruiting Process

Although their salary recommendations have not always been followed by the president and the Congress, the quadrennial commissions have made other important contributions to our understanding of the compensation issue in government. Recent commission members have been of uniformly high quality, drawn from the top ranks of business, labor, universities, and law. In 1976 the commission had the assistance of a top-flight staff drawn from some of the major corporations in the country. In addition, Dr. Arnold Weber, then provost at Carnegie-Mellon University, prepared a special study for the commission on the role of compensation in determining why people do or do not go into or stay in government service. The 1980 commission staff was drawn from the government sector. Its work was supplemented by a detailed analysis by highly regarded management consultants, Hay Associates. Both commissions produced impressive reports with solidly based recommendations.

Based on a survey for the 1976 commission on past and present government officials and some who declined to come into government, Dr. Weber found that although compensation does not operate to the exclusion of other factors in decisions about accepting appointments, it "is likely to exert a significant influence."[8] By 1980 the commission took a harder line, describing what it called "a quiet crisis." The commission concluded: "There is growing evidence that low salaries are a major reason for highly talented people declining appointment to key positions in the Federal government."[9] Based on the Weber data, the 1976 commission concluded that compensation plays an even more significant role in the decision to leave government than in the decision to come into government. Both commissions expressed grave concern that the continued refusal to grant needed salary increases might lead us toward a government of the rich, the young, and the inexperienced.

Both commissions further argued that parity with the private sector is an inappropriate and unnecessary objective. As the 1976 commission pointed out, comparability is of little value in determining salaries for top federal political executives.[10] It is hardly enlightening to attempt to find jobs that compare with those of secretary of defense or secretary of health and human services. No private sector executives have responsibility for such massive budgets and such obstinate problems. Even if a salary comparison could be made, for example, between running the Defense Department and running General Motors, it would have little meaning. What the commissions call the "psychic income" of government service—the challenge of working on the world's toughest problems, the prestige of public service, the potential future opportunities—makes most people willing to accept some financial sacrifice. The survey by Dr. Weber for the 1976 commission found that the average senior official accepted a decrease in salary of just over 21 percent in entering federal government service. In some cases the financial sacrifice is extraordinary. Some cabinet secretaries recruited from the top ranks of major corporations have had to give up salaries several times larger than what they would earn as public officials.

The 1976 commission concluded that pay should be established at a rate adequate to attract to government people of outstanding ability who do not have additional sources of income and to make it possible for them to devote full time to their jobs. According to the commission: "Americans do not want someone seeking high government posts because of the good salary, nor do they want able people to turn down the job because the salary is too low."[11]

Both commissions emphasized the importance of not allowing compensation to deteriorate substantially during the course of government service. In his study for the 1976 commission, Dr. Weber found that decisions to leave government were directly linked to economic erosion while in government service.

The commissions both concluded that the difference in pay may be wider as one moves up the Executive Level scale because of the greater relative psychic income at the cabinet level. In fact, in accordance with commission recommendations, increases in recent years have been less for cabinet secretaries than for the subcabinet.

Both commissions recommended abandoning linkage between Congress, Executive Level II, and the judges of the courts of appeals. The rationale for linkage is political rather than substantive, and neither commission found any persuasive reasons for maintaining it.

Both commissions also recommended that legislation be enacted to allow reimbursement of relocation costs for newly appointed federal executives. They recognized that the cost of moving to Washington can be a significant deterrent. According to a survey cited by the 1980 commission, major U.S. corporations provide at least some relocation benefits to 99 percent of newly hired professionals. The Civil Service Reform Act of 1978 permits payment of certain relocation costs of newly hired members of the Senior Executive Service. Recommendations for reimbursing federal political executives for their moving expenses were made as early as 1963 by the Advisory Panel on Federal Salary System. None, however, has yet been enacted.

The problem of compensation for federal executives, although more complex than is generally understood, remains a substantial one. Low salaries do not prevent the federal government from recruiting a good many able people. Fortunately, public service has a number of attractions that outweigh salary concerns for a number of presidential appointees. But, as recent quadrennial commissions have indicated, inadequate salaries are a barrier to recruiting from among one group of especially desirable candidates for government service: those highly trained technicians and midcareer managers whose expertise, energy, and creativity has been amply demonstrated in the private sector. By helping to remove this key group from the recruiting pool, inadequate salaries have a negative effect on the nation's capacity to govern effectively. And by inhibiting the movement of talented people from the private sector into the public service, low salaries help to build walls of misunderstanding between the government and the private sector. If the gap between public and private salaries continues to grow, increasing numbers of the best people in the private sector will find it financially infeasible to accept an appointment in the executive branch of the federal government. We think that a troublesome prospect.

SUMMARY

The job of a public executive is demanding and difficult. It can be rife with frustrations and aggravations. But it can also be a source of great personal satisfaction and unmatched opportunity for American citizens to make important contributions to their country. Our concern here is with the ability of the president to recruit and retain the services of talented Americans. We believe that ability will be enhanced when two things happen.

First, we believe a more balanced portrait of the character of public service must be drawn by the communications media and by that large group of present and former presidential appointees who have found their government experience stimulating and valuable. Until there are more effective efforts to display the positive side of the federal executive work environment, perceptions in the private sector will continue to be unduly colored by the stories of frustration and dismay that seem to compose the majority of journalistic coverage of this issue.

Second, stronger measures must be undertaken, especially by those who manage the appointment process, to improve the work environment for presidential appointees and to ease the transition from the private sector into government jobs. This requires greater attention to the adequacy of compensation levels, the problem of appointee burnout, the needs of spouses and families, and the tasks of transition and orientation of new appointees. In each of these areas there is much that can be done to correct and overcome the negative perception of the federal work environment that poses a current handicap to presidential recruitment efforts.

NOTES

1. Hugh Sidey, "The Joy of Governing," *Time*, October 4, 1982.
2. John G. Kemeny, Compton Lecture, Massachusetts Institute of Technology, April 11, 1980.
3. As quoted in Philip M. Boffey, "Carlucci: Thoughts on Government and Leaving It," *New York Times*, January 4, 1983.
4. Sander Vanocur, "Political Values and Trends," *Change and Governance: Some Strategy Choices* (Washington, D.C.: National Association of State Budget Officers, January 1980), p. 81.

5. Daniel Yankelovich, *New Rules: Searching for Self-Fulfillment in a World Turned Upside Down* (New York: Random House, 1981), p. 184.
6. A. Bartlett Giamatti, *The University and the Public Interest* (New York: Atheneum, 1981), p. 168.
7. "The Too-High Price of Public Service," *Fortune*, December 1977.
8. U.S. Commission on Executive, Legislative and Judicial Salaries, *Report of the Commission on Executive, Legislative and Judicial Salaries* (Washington, D.C.: U.S. Government Printing Office, 1976), p. 38. Dr. Weber's study, "Compensation and Federal Executive Service: Survey and Analysis," is printed in U.S. Commission on Executive, Legislative and Judicial Salaries, *Staff Report to the Commission on Executive, Legislative and Judicial Salaries* (Washington, D.C.: U.S. Government Printing Office, 1977).
9. U.S. Commission on Executive, Legislative and Judicial Salaries, *Report of the Commission on Executive, Legislative, and Judicial Salaries* (Washington, D.C.: U.S. Government Printing Office, 1980), pp. ix and 1.
10. For a discussion of the difficulties in using comparability concepts in making compensation adjustments for federal executives, see Wesley R. Liebtag, "A Private Sector Approach to Federal Executive Compensation: Illumination or Illusion?" in Robert W. Hartman and Arnold R. Weber, eds., *The Rewards of Public Service* (Washington, D.C.: Brookings Institution, 1980), pp. 141-62.
11. U.S. Commission on Executive, Legislative and Judicial Salaries, *Report of the Commission on Executive, Legislative and Judicial Salaries* (1976), p. 32.

Chapter 5

CONFLICT OF INTEREST
The Reality and the Perception

Few issues in our politics are thornier or more controversial than the matter of public ethics. The American people expect their public servants to satisfy the highest standards of integrity in the performance of their official responsibilities. It is their strong desire that public decisions be made in the public interest, without bias for or against any single or special interest and without regard to the consequences of those decisions for the financial status of the decision-makers themselves.

Attention to this concern has become especially acute in the past two decades and has resulted in the enactment of several new and stringent additions to federal ethics requirements. Anyone entering upon appointive public service must comply with these requirements as a condition of employment. They are part of the fabric of modern administrative life.

There is growing concern, however, that these efforts to improve the integrity of public decisionmaking have a dark side and that they are becoming a barrier to the recruitment of able people into the public service. Too many prospective appointees now believe that submission to conflict of interest requirements is too high a price to pay for the opportunity to serve one's country as a government executive. Is that a correct perception?

In this chapter we will explore the impact of the conflict of interest issue. We will identify the important elements of current laws and regulations, and we will examine common perceptions—and misperceptions—of the problems they create for presidential appointees. Our purpose here is to get an accurate fix on the role that conflict of interest rules have come to play in the appointment process. Are they a genuine recruiting problem? If so, can a better balance be struck between the need to ensure the integrity of government decisions and the need to keep the door to public service open to competent and creative people?

CURRENT CONFLICT OF INTEREST REQUIREMENTS

Some of our present conflict of interest laws trace back to criminal statutes enacted in the middle of the nineteenth century. Acting on advice provided in a 1960 study by the Association of the Bar of the City of New York, the Kennedy administration in 1962 recommended, and the Congress approved, an extensive codification of these laws. In 1965 standards for ethical conduct by executive branch officers and employees were further codified in Executive Order No. 11222, issued by President Lyndon Johnson. In 1978 Congress enacted the Ethics in Government Act which further refined conflict of interest standards and established the Office of Government Ethics (OGE) in the Office of Personnel Management to oversee the compliance of federal officials with these laws. Three important components of these requirements have a direct impact on the recruitment of federal executives.

Substantive Conflicts of Interest

Fundamental to the conflict of interest laws are restrictions on participation in an official capacity in matters in which the official or spouse, dependent children, partner, or organization has a financial interest. An appointee could not, for instance, award a government contract to a company in which he or she owns stock.

Appointees are also prohibited from receiving any supplementation of salary from any nongovernment source for services to the federal government. They may receive severance payments from a former corporate employer, but only if those are made pursuant to formal company policy in recognition of prior service to the company. Appointees may also receive pensions and health and other benefits from former employers if those have been established in good faith in the normal course of business.

One other significant restriction is the prohibition imposed on federal officials against representing anyone other than the government on matters that involve the interests of the government in a direct and substantial way. A former lobbyist for an interest group, appointed to a position in the subcabinet, for example, could not serve as that group's advocate in government decisions affecting that group's interests.

Postemployment Restrictions

Title V of the Ethics in Government Act expanded previous restrictions on the postemployment activities of former government officials. It maintained without change the lifetime prohibition against representing anyone before the government in a matter involving specific parties that a former official had handled personally and substantially while in the government. For example, an official who reviewed and approved a city's application for federal assistance for an urban renewal project would be barred from subsequently representing the city in relation to that project.

The 1978 act also extended from one year to two years the prohibition on involvement of a former government employee in a matter that had been under his or her official responsibility while in government service, and it added a prohibition against high-ranking former officials representing anyone before their former agencies for one year after leaving government service. The act went a step further, prohibiting former officials not only from representing anyone before their former agencies for a year but also from advising or assisting people who had dealings with those agencies.

This last provision posed real barriers to recruitment from such categories as lawyers, college professors, and interest group leaders and was an immediate target of criticism. It was amended in 1979 so that it is now rarely applicable.

Public Financial Disclosure

Beginning in 1965, top federal officials were required to report information about their personal finances. This requirement was not imposed on all presidential appointees, nor did it mandate public disclosure. Financial disclosure reports were sent to the chairman of the Civil Service Commission, who was instructed to keep them confidential but to inform the president whenever he believed the potential for conflict of interest to exist.

Title II of the Ethics in Government Act broadened this provision to cover all federal executives and to require them to disclose publicly the personal financial information they reported. Senior government employees, including all presidential appointees, must now complete the Executive Personnel Financial Disclosure Report (SF 278) which is then available for public inspection. In this report they must indicate in detail such information as existing financial relationships with any corporation, partnership, or other institution; names of creditors; a list of all interests in real property; a listing of all sources of income; all significant assets and liabilities; and affiliations with any organizations that might be relevant to matters of conflict of interest. In addition to providing all this information on themselves, appointees must provide similar information for their spouses and dependent children.

Appointees are not required to provide copies of their income tax returns or to file a net worth statement. And, with the exception of personal earned income, information is listed by category of amount. There are six categories; assets under $1,000 are exempted, and the top category is "over $250,000." Disclosure requirements are limited to all income-producing assets. For example, assets held for investment must be reported, but personal jewelry or primary residences need not.

PUBLIC PERCEPTIONS AND CRITICISMS

Although the federal government now has an extensive set of conflict of interest requirements, debate over them is far from closed. In a general sense, that debate is structured around two opposing points of view. One holds that the conflict of interest laws are a moderate and reasonable approach to a troubling national concern. If the American people are to regain confidence in the propriety and legitimacy of government actions, they must have assurance that those actions are undertaken in the public interest. Conflict of interest laws afford them some such assurance.

The other side sees the conflict of interest laws as much too severe for the purpose they are intended to serve, that is, as a kind of overkill that impedes presidential recruitment of successful people from the private sector. This side holds that acceptable protections against conflict of interest can easily be created that cause much less harm to the process of getting the best possible people into government.

Degree of Disclosure

The debate is waged on a number of fronts. A major target of criticism is the requirement for public financial disclosure. Opponents of financial disclosure argue that it is an unnecessary and improper invasion of privacy. They fear that it creates opportunities for the news media, interest groups, and political rivals to use this information against appointees. They argue that making this information public does little to enhance protections against conflict of interest and that the public interest would be just as well served if this information were only provided to appropriate officials in the executive branch.

Critics also suggest that the disclosure requirements are more detailed and penetrating than the public interest warrants. They find no rationale for the establishment of multiple categories for reporting the value of financial assets and holdings. Jonathan C. Rose, an assistant attorney general for legal policy in the Reagan administration, recently made this point. "The question," he noted, "is whether there is or is not a conflict. Why quantify the amount? If you are over the cliff by one inch, it's the same as being over by five feet. We should eliminate the voyeuristic approach to calculating people's net worth."[1]

Critics of this requirement also take umbrage at its inclusion of relatives of public officials. They argue that relatives are innocent bystanders in this process and that, since they are not themselves entering public service, the public has no right to information about their finances.

For each of these criticisms, however, proponents of the ethics laws have a counter. To the argument that public disclosure is unnecessary, they respond with the suggestion that public disclosure enhances the likelihood of strong enforcement. Public disclosure, in their view, has forced public officials who must disclose and those responsible for monitoring disclosure to take the conflict of interest laws more seriously than they had in the past. Public disclosure, as they see it, adds an important measure of accountability to the process of preventing conflicts of interest. They note as well that state and federal courts have upheld public disclosure laws against a variety of constitutional and other challenges, that for the most part the news media have been responsible in their use of disclosed information, and that expressed fears that public disclosure would be an invitation to theft and kidnapping have not materialized. Proponents also note that the requirements imposed on relatives of federal officials are essential to cover all possible conflicts of interest; that they only cover these persons specified in substantive conflict of interest laws; and that they require only the source of earned income, not the amount, to be disclosed.

Proponents of the conflict of interest regulations also support the use of broad categories for reporting the value of an asset or holding. They point out that this represents a compromise between those who think that no amounts need be reported and those who think that exact amounts should be disclosed. They believe it is appropriate for officials to indicate the magnitude of their holdings because it is often as important to know the extent of a potential conflict as it is simply to recognize its existence.

On one matter there is agreement between those who question and those who support the current conflict of interest requirements. That is an almost universal criticism of the redundant reporting requirements that the Ethics in Government Act, the White House, and the Senate committees impose on presidential appointees who require confirmation. Many committees have their own reporting requirements and often these are different from those used throughout the executive branch. Even within the executive branch, different forms are used by the White House and by the OGE. This not only means that nominees must go through the disclosure process twice, but it also tends to add to the time it takes to get them confirmed and on the job. The only apparent reason for the inconsistency of reporting requirements is force of habit and, in the Senate, a commitment to committee autonomy. It is difficult to find any public interest that is served by this.

Removing Real Conflicts

Some critics believe that restrictions on financial holdings and on relationships with former employers too often make it cumbersome and expensive to enter government service, especially for those in the middle of their careers in large private sector organizations.

While there are few cases in which steps cannot be taken to achieve compliance with these requirements, the critics note that the costs of doing so are often substantial—enough so in some instances to deter talented people from accepting presidential appointments. One cost is that incurred when a prospective official holds stock that poses a potential conflict of interest. In some cases, the cure for that kind of conflict is divestiture. But this may come at a time when the value of the stock is low and selling it would cause a financial loss to the individual. Conversely, a sale of stock may reap substantial capital gains for the owner, but, with little time for financial planning, heavy capital gains taxes may ensue. Nothing in current federal law protects prospective government officials from the heavy tax burden they may encounter in divesting of financial assets in order to comply with conflict of interest requirements.

Another cost often identified by critics of the conflict of interest laws is that which midcareer people encounter when they are forced, as they often are, to sever their relationship with their private sector employers. For many this means more than just the reduction in salary described in the previous chapter. It may also mean removal from a health benefit and pension plan, the loss of valuable stock options, and, perhaps most distressing of all, the loss of upward mobility within a corporation and the long-term career consequences that implies.

Proponents of the conflict of interest requirements recognize the costs these sometimes impose but believe that they are outweighed by the beneficial way in which these laws serve the public interest. They further note that the conflict of interest requirements are not so draconian as some critics and some potential appointees believe them to be. They point out that divestiture is not the only possible cure for most substantive conflicts of interest, that in fact it is rarely required, and that other cures generally can be found that are far less costly to appointees. While regretting the fact that some appointees must suffer financial sacrifices in complying with conflict of interest laws—and that a very small number simply cannot comply—they regard those sacrifices as an inevitable consequence of ensuring the integrity of public servants.

Life After Government Service

The restrictions placed on executives after they leave government are designed to prevent the government from serving as a "revolving door" for self-interested individuals and the special interests they may represent. By restricting the postemployment activities of federal officials, especially their immediate postemployment activities, the likelihood of appointees abusing their government service for personal gain should be reduced. The proponents of these restrictions believe that they are a reasonable and moderate set of constraints that accomplish their objectives.

Critics disagree. In their view, postemployment restrictions are a major source of the uncertainty that prospective appointees often experience when they are offered a presidential appointment. For those who do not intend to stay in government for more than a few years, postemployment possibilities are a significant concern. If they believe, as many do, that those opportunities will be limited when their government service is over, they may be reluctant to leave the private sector at all. Since appointees are often recruited from, and hope to return to, industries that have a direct relationship with the agency in which they will serve in government, the reason for this concern is readily apparent.

The critics often worry that postemployment restrictions are a threat to the American tradition of leadership provided by people who are not career government employees but who are willing to serve for short periods of time when their services are needed. If we make it difficult for these people to get out of the government, the critics argue, we should also recognize that we are making it difficult to get them into government in the first place. The decision to accept a presidential appointment, in this view, is likely to be closely related to the opportunities that exist when that appointment terminates.

The proponents of postemployment restrictions recognize that such fears exist but believe that they are magnified out of proportion. In reality, they point out, the postemployment restrictions are not very constraining and almost never prevent an appointee from going back to the private sector employer from which he was recruited. At most, there may be some modest restriction on the activities in which that individual can participate immediately after leaving government service. The proponents also note, with ample supporting evidence, that most former appointees have little trouble finding very good—and often very lucrative—jobs when they leave the government. The normal experience, they suggest, is that government service provides a boost to career advancement and earning power and that the vast majority of appointees leave the government for much higher paying jobs than they had when they entered.

IMPACT ON PRESIDENTIAL RECRUITING

Conflict of interest regulations are a source of significant consternation to both potential appointees and presidential recruiters. There are several reasons for this. One is the reality that we now have a rigorous and demanding set of restrictions on the personal financial activities of public officials. Conflict of interest is not a matter that the federal government takes lightly, and for some public servants the requirements of the law do indeed impose real—and, in a few cases, costly—constraints on private financial activities. Some of our public servants have had to bear the brunt of the costs of the American people's demand for high ethical standards in government. Others, given the opportunity to do so, have declined to serve.

A second source of consternation over these laws and regulations is that they are written with a degree of intentional imprecision that sometimes begets misinterpretation. Obviously, no conflict of interest requirement could be written to cover the financial and employment situation of every potential public executive. No two cases are ever exactly the same; some are extraordinarily complex. To cover all of these personal situations, the laws leave a good deal of discretion to those who implement the conflict of interest requirements.

That imprecision in the laws, combined with an absence of informed understanding in the press and the public of how those laws work, has been a major source of misperception about conflict of interest issues. While it is true that those laws sometimes do impose significant constraints on people entering public service for the first time, it is also true that the extent of those impositions is often overestimated. The conflict of interest regulations do *not* require the divestiture of all financial holdings that pose a potential conflict; they do *not* mandate total severance in every case from a previous employer; they do *not* significantly curtail postemployment opportunities; and they do *not* require publication of every aspect of an appointee's financial condition. Yet, uninformed public opinion often seems to assume that they do all of these things, without exception and without mercy. This pattern of misunderstanding is, for obvious reasons, a burden on presidential recruiting efforts, especially in the private sector.

That burden is compounded by presidential recruiters who sometimes fail themselves fully to understand conflict of interest requirements, who are unprepared to cope with them in the recruiting process, and who are unable to assuage the fears of potential appointees. The Reagan experience is instructive in this regard. Pendleton James, the head of the Reagan personnel office, readily admitted: "I found out too late about the new laws we had to live under in the appointment process."[2] Later he said, "I had overlooked the Act, overlooked it because I frankly wasn't aware of the extent that it would affect our appointments."[3] As long as those who need to be most familiar with conflict of interest requirements are themselves uncertain, there is little likelihood that the misperception that prevails in the public and the press will soon dissipate.

MAKING CONFLICT OF INTEREST LAWS WORKABLE: "CURES" UNDER THE LAW

An important reason for the fear that conflict of interest laws sometimes generate in the hearts of prospective appointees is a failure to understand the range of possibilities available for curing potential conflicts of interest. It is important to remember that these laws were not enacted in order to prevent able people from serving in government. Instead, their highest purpose was to secure the integrity of the government's decisionmaking process. They were established to provide standards for identifying potential conflicts of interest and to create mechanisms to prevent potential conflicts from standing in the way of individuals who were willing to serve the government in a noncareer capacity. The conflict of interest laws, regulations, and practices establish several approaches for avoiding conflicts of interest.

Disqualification

When an appointee accepts a position in which there is a remote chance of acting in a matter that poses a conflict of interest, that appointee may agree to be disqualified from participation in that matter. In cases where the likelihood of such a situation occurring is indeed small, this can be an acceptable cure for a potential conflict of interest. It is a reasonable approach to this problem and has been widely employed.

If, however, an appointee takes a post in which a number of matters under his or her jurisdiction may pose a conflict of this sort, disqualification is likely to be an inadequate remedy. The appointee would be so often excluded from important decisions as to be unable to perform an effective public service. Hence, disqualification is a tool of limited utility when a potential conflict of interest would occur freqently.

Waivers

Another cure that may be employed when a financial holding that poses a potential conflict of interest is small in value is for the officer with authority to do so to grant a waiver of the conflict of interest requirements. Under the law, this may be done in cases where the financial interest is "not so substantial as to be deemed likely to affect the integrity of the services which the government may expect from such officer or employee." The authority to grant waivers is vested in cabinet secretaries and agency heads for executives under their jurisdiction. The president has the authority to grant waivers for cabinet secretaries; under provisions of executive orders and White House regulations of long standing, however, that authority is delegated to the White House counsel.

In practice, waivers have not often been employed as remedies for conflicts of interest. In part, this reflects the difficulty that sometimes occurs in making a factual determination in advance about the extent to which a financial interest, even a relatively small one, is likely to pose a conflict. The more important reason, however, for the reluctance to grant waivers is the fear of political repercussions. Officials have been cautious about this—perhaps more cautious than the public interest requires—in order to avoid criticism for treating potential conflicts too casually.

Blind Trusts

Since a conflict of interest cannot effectively occur if officials do not know they are acting in a way that enhances the value of their holdings, one remedy for conflicts of interest is the establishment of a blind trust. Under the Ethics in Government Act, an acceptable blind trust is one for which there is a truly independent trustee, an approved set of assets, and a trust instrument meeting minimum standards specified in the law. Fundamental to the theory of a blind trust is that the government official not know what financial interests are included in the trust so that he or she cannot knowingly make decisions that will increase the value of those interests. The establishment of blind trusts is overseen by the OGE, which has primary responsibility for certifying their "blindness."

Blind trusts have long been used as a remedy for conflicts of interest in the federal government, but only since the passage of the Ethics in Government Act have there been statutory or regulatory standards for their proper formulation. In spite of that, however, they are not yet a widely employed cure for conflicts of interest. Data from mid-1982 indicate, for instance, that of the several hundred individuals appointed by the Reagan administration, just over a score had established blind trusts.[4]

Divestiture

The surest cure for a potential conflict of interest is to eliminate the financial interest that causes it. In the case of stock holdings—the most common source of potential conflicts—that implies divestiture. Though sometimes Senate committees impose such a requirement as a condition of confirmation, nowhere do the conflict of interest statutes mandate the divestiture of holdings that pose a potential conflict of interest. Appointees may find, however, that none of the other remedies available to them will satisfactorily protect them against possible charges of conflict of interest.

Divestiture is a troublesome remedy in several ways. First, it may cause individuals to sell stocks that have been in their or their family's possession for some time and thus have sentimental as well as financial significance. Second, divestiture may require a substantial sacrifice if the value of the stock happens to be below its value at the time it was purchased or well below what its value will become in the future. Even if the stock is worth considerably more than it was at the time it was acquired, divestiture may incur heavy capital gains taxes, all occurring in one tax year.

Though divestiture is the most complete of the cures for conflict of interest, it is employed very rarely, and then only as a last resort by individuals who abhor the costs it imposes but who see no other way to prevent the appearance of conflict of interest.

Leaves of Absence

Those appointees who are entering government service from the private sector and who do not wish to completely sever relationships with their former employers may be able, under certain conditions, to arrange for a leave of absence. The conflict of interest laws do not make any absolute requirement that an employee must sever all relationships with a former employer. When a leave of absence can be arranged that does not create a prohibited financial interest (as defined in 18 U.S.C. 208–209) or the appearance thereof, this may be an acceptable way for an employee to maintain a relationship with a former employer. There are at any given time a number of presidential appointees who are on leaves of absence from the private sector. To date, that possibility has been more widely pursued by university professors than by any other group of appointees.

It is also possible within the scope of the conflict of interest laws for individuals to continue to participate in pension, group health insurance, and other good faith benefit plans established in the normal course of business and maintained by their former employers. This may be done, with or without a formal leave of absence, with the approval of designated agency ethics officials and the OGE.

SUMMARY

It is unlikely that all Americans will ever be completely happy with the measures we adopt to ensure the integrity of our public officials. There will continue to be people who think those measures are too weak and people who think they are too stringent. Debate on this issue is not closed, nor will it be soon.

Our purpose in this chapter has been neither to applaud the existing conflict of interest regulations nor to offer a detailed critique. Our interest is only with their impact on presidential personnel recruiting. Our finding has been that the public perception of the federal conflict of interest laws is an impediment to presidential recruiting. We are not able to determine the precise magnitude of the barriers created by the conflict of interest laws themselves, because of the difficulty in counting or identifying potential presidential appointees who refused even to be considered for appointment because they did not want to get entangled in conflict of interest controversies. We do know, however, from our own interviews and from the frequent testimony of presidential personnel recruiters, that conflict of interest issues are a significant complication to recruiting efforts. President Reagan's assistant for personnel, Pendleton James, has stated publicly that "literally hundreds" of candidates for positions below the cabinet level lost interest when they learned about the conflict of interest requirements.[5]

Our examination of the issue has also indicated that much of the fear that conflict of interest requirements inspire in prospective appointees results from misunderstanding of what those laws actually require and an absence of information about the several mechanisms they permit for curing potential conflicts of interest. Indeed, we have been struck by the pervasive haze of ignorance that seems to enshroud public discourse on conflict of interest issues.

If the constraints these requirements currently impose on the appointment process are to be mitigated, two steps will have to be taken. First, some real and practical problems in the conflict of interest laws must be corrected. Among those are the excessive number of financial reporting categories mandated by public financial disclosure requirements, the tax burden imposed on officials who are forced to divest themselves of stock holdings, the complexity and redundancy of disclosure forms, and the reluctance of federal officials to grant waivers for inconsequential financial holdings. For each of these problems, we will recommend specific corrective action in the final chapter of this book.

We believe, however, that more than that is necessary to overcome the constraints that conflict of interest laws currently impose on presidential recruiting. Those constraints will begin to disappear only when public perceptions of those laws are clarified and corrected. The press, the leaders of affected interest groups, and presidential recruiters themselves all have an obligation here to improve their own understanding of these laws and to convey a clearer picture than they currently do to prospective appointees. Until that occurs, the price that we pay as a nation to ensure the integrity of our public officials will be higher than it needs to be.

NOTES

1. Quoted in Dick Kirschten, "Why Not the Best?" *National Journal* 14 (June 12, 1982): 1064.
2. Statement by E. Pendleton James at a panel on "Staffing the Reagan Presidency," American Political Science Association Convention, New York City, September 2, 1981.
3. Quoted in U.S. Office of Government Ethics, *Proceedings of the Third Annual Conference, 1982* (Washington, D.C.: OGE, May 1983), p. 43.
4. Arlene Hershman, "They Put Their Trust in Blind Trust," *Dun's Business Month*, May 1982, pp. 42–49.
5. Quoted in Kirschten, "Why Not the Best?" p. 1064.

Chapter 6

RECOMMENDATIONS

Our investigation of the presidential appointment process has uncovered much to admire in that process. We have been impressed with many of the efforts made by recent administrations to improve the scope and care of their recruitment efforts. We believe that, on balance, the public interest has been well served in the past decade by the renewal of the national commitment to high ethical standards for its public officials. And we have been pleased that so many of the people we have encountered in our investigation possess a genuine understanding of the importance of presidential appointments and a profound concern for the effectiveness of the process by which they are made.

But we have also found many characteristics of the appointment process that are not satisfactory, that detract from the successful recruitment and deployment of able noncareer executives and thus diminish the performance capabilities of the federal government. We believe there is much still to be done, in the short term and in the long term, to improve the appointment process and thereby ensure a steady flow of talent into the highest levels of government.

BROADENING OF TALENT SOURCES FOR PRESIDENTIAL APPOINTMENTS

Problem

Recent presidential administrations have failed to tap effectively all of the sources of managerial and technical talent that are available to them. In part, this results from the problems in establishing effective recruiting mechanisms. There is, however, a deeper set of problems at the root of this—problems that deserve the attention and concerted corrective efforts of people inside and outside of government who are concerned about the quality of government management and decisionmaking.

We believe that able, creative, and experienced people are the most important ingredient in the recipe for good government. We also believe that the talents for which the federal government has the greatest need are scattered throughout our society, often in places outside the political mainstream from which most government recruiting takes place. To increase the flow of those people into public service, three important conditions are necessary. One is the existence of a public sector environment that is hospitable to creative and competent people. The second is a dedicated commitment by the president and his personnel staff to find and recruit those people. The third is a willingness on the part of those people to make themselves available and to prepare themselves for effective public service.

We believe there is much that can be done within the private sector and in cooperative efforts between the private and public sector to heighten interest in presidential appointments and to improve the quality of preparation for them.

Recommendation 1

Persistent attacks on the federal civil service reduce presidential opportunities for effective leadership and seriously diminish the prospects for attracting good people into government employment. To avoid this, campaign rhetoric by presidential candidates should aim not to denigrate and undermine the significant contributions of career civil servants but to encourage, inspire, and challenge them to effective performance in the national interest.

One of the problems that has been brought to our attention throughout this inquiry is the harmful impact on presidential recruiting efforts caused by negative public attitudes about government and public life. Almost everywhere in the United States, but especially in the business community, there is a sense that public life is corrosive, demeaning, and unrewarding. The intractability of public problems, the difficulty in building national consensus, the jugular instincts of the news media, and the craven pursuit of political influence by special interests have all been repeatedly cited to us as perceived characteristics of contemporary government operations. The public opinion polls that we have examined suggest consistently that many Americans have little confidence in the federal government's ability to solve the problems that most trouble them or in the integrity and competence of public officials.

The negative consensus we have found in public attitudes about government has many sources. We have not attempted to identify them all. One, however—the rhetoric of leading politicians—was so often and so disparagingly cited that we believe it is worth discussing here. It appears to be an unfortunate fact of contemporary politics that there is no safer statement, no surer applause line for a candidate than a withering criticism of the government in Washington and those who operate it. Congressmen, we are told, run against the Congress. Presidential candidates run against the federal bureaucracy. Political speeches are full of broad denunciations of the laziness, isolation, and venality of public servants. No names are named, but the indictments are sweeping.

There is a certain said irony in the fact that presidents themselves contribute to many of the problems their recruiters encounter. By helping to lower the esteem in which public servants are held, they participate in the creation of an inhospitable recruiting environment.

This is self-defeating. The simple fact is that prospective appointees in the private sector will not be anxious to join a government that is distrusted by the people it serves. So long as American political leaders feed that distrust with their rhetoric, recruiting will remain an unnecessarily difficult task.

We readily admit that we have no simple solution to this problem. Negative attitudes once established are hard to change. Campaign tactics once successful are hard to stop. We recognize that neither will be swept away by a broad brush of exhortation by us. We believe it is important, however, for us to identify the very harmful impact that these negative attitudes about government and public servants have had on presidential recruitment efforts and to express our hope for a change in the tone of political discourse on this issue. We find little benefit to the nation, or its presidents, from the unspecified, *ad hominem* attacks on the federal government and its employees that have been so prominently featured in recent national campaigns. Recruiting opportunities will improve when they end.

Recommendation 2

The leaders of private sector organizations (corporations, communications media, labor unions, law firms, universities, interest groups) should encourage their best employees to undertake periods of public service and should assist them in doing so when opportunities arise.

We have been distressed throughout the course of this study at the lack of support that leaders in the private sector have given to their employees who were candidates for presidential appointments. They have often discouraged them from accepting these appointments because of their own negative feelings about government and because they were unhappy at the prospect of losing the skills of able employees, even if only for a short time, to the government. We think this is a regrettable and shortsighted attitude that harms our nation directly and substantially. It is regrettable because it contributes to the government's difficulty in recruiting talented people. It is shortsighted because we believe that the private sector has as much to gain when its people take noncareer positions in the government as does the public sector.

If we are to break down the animus that continues to exist in this country between government and business—and we must if we are to confront successfully the challenges of the present and the future—we must first diminish the misunderstanding on which that animus is often based. We can think of no better way to do that than to encourage the movement of people between the private and public sector. Our system of government assumes significant contributions from the "in-and-outers." Government decisionmaking benefits from the moderating influences of those who understand the impacts of those decisions. Hostility in the private sector is mollified by a clearer sense of the complex set of forces to which government decisions must respond. When the leaders of private sector organizations help open the doors to this kind of personnel interchange, they serve both public and private interests.

Recommendation 3

Programs that provide exposure to and experiences in government for people from the private sector should be increased in number and expanded in size.

We often asked the people we interviewed what can be done to improve a president's range of choices in staffing his administration. One of the responses we heard most frequently was that people whose careers will be spent primarily in the private sector should be exposed to and given opportunities to acquire experience in the public service early in their lives. This should cultivate their interest and better prepare them for service at high levels. There currently exist a number of fellowship programs designed for this purpose. Of these, the White House Fellowships are perhaps the best known. These are a useful model for providing the kind of early interest and training that may later contribute to the recruitment of a valuable public servant.

We believe that other models might also be employed for this purpose. These would include work, even part-time or volunteer work, in state and local government; pro bono or per diem service on federal advisory commissions; participation in joint public-private studies of critical issues; and hands-on internships for students. To get the best we can from our government executives, we need to encourage programs of this sort to help them prepare for the responsibilities they will confront as presidential appointees.

Recommendation 4

Law, business, and other professional schools should provide some preparation for the opportunities in government that their students may wish to pursue.

We believe that professional schools can play an important part in lowering the barriers that now exist between the public and private sectors of our society. Most graduates of professional schools will spend the bulk of their working lives in the private sector. All of them, however, will be affected by government decisions, and many of them will have opportunities at some points in their lives to participate in those decisions. Some will serve terms as noncareer executives in the federal government.

We believe that some basic preparation in the operations of the federal government and in the techniques of working successfully in a governmental environment can usefully be included in the curricula of many professional schools, including government internships, lectureships, public servants in residence programs, and so on. We would hope as well that professional educators will recognize the value of this not only for their students but for the nation as well. We believe that the long-term interests of the United States will be well served when we have a talented corps of national leaders who are at home in both the private and the public sector. And we believe that our professional schools can contribute mightily to the establishment of that pool of talent.

Recommendation 5

Presidents should draw more heavily on the career civil service as a valuable source of presidential appointees.

It is ironic that presidential recruiters often overlook one of the country's most fertile sources of potential presidential appointees: the career civil service. We are familiar with the concerns expressed by some about the possibility of "infecting" career executives by putting them in policymaking positions. We have heard the argument that appointments are "wasted" on career civil servants because the government already has their services. We do not find much merit in either argument. Career civil servants have demonstrated repeatedly that they can move in and out of appointive positions without undermining the quality or objectivity of their future service to the government. We find nothing wasteful about elevating a talented career employee to a high-level executive position in which the full extent of his or her abilities can be utilized.

We believe there are several very good reasons for presidents to increase the number of appointees they draw from the career services. One is simply that there are many able and creative individuals among the more than 2 million civilian employees of the federal government. This is one of our richest talent resources, and it is self-defeating to disregard it.

Another advantage of this is that the civil service is an important repository of the government's institutional memory. An experienced civil servant, elevated to a position as a presidential appointee, brings a unique measure of knowledge and experience to that position. Continuity is enhanced by this since the learning curve for a civil servant will invariably be shorter than that for a government novice recruited from the private sector. A president anxious to "hit the ground running," as most suggest they are, will find it an advantage to select some career civil servants to accompany him. They know the trail well.

Finally, we believe that fuller use of career civil servants in appointive positions would be an excellent motivator for all of the career services. If competent career officials could have some real hope that there might be opportunities at some time in their careers to step into senior appointive positions, this would be a powerful incentive for them to perform at a level of proficiency that demonstrated their qualifications for those positions.

APPOINTMENT AND CONFIRMATION PROCEDURES

Problem

The appointment process is really two processes, not one. The first operates during the transition period, when a new administration is trying to establish itself in Washington. Recent experience affords ample testimony to the difficulty in doing this. Those who assist the president in selecting the personnel for his administration rarely start early enough to prepare for the onslaught that comes after the election. They are understaffed. They often do not understand the nature of all of the positions they have to fill; sometimes they have difficulty simply identifying those positions. They become so overwhelmed with job applications that they have little time to conduct searches for the kinds of candidates they most desire. Because their procedures for clearing and investigating candidates are not fully established, frustrating delays occur in getting executive positions filled. Typically, much of the first year of a president's term has elapsed before all of his appointees are in place. With little carry-over of process or institutional memory from previous presidencies, each new administration must build an appointments operation from scratch. Misjudgments, oversights, and delays are a common result.

The second phase of the appointment process occurs after the transition and during the rest of an administration. The personnel staff can begin to establish routines that allow it to exercise more care in selecting appointees than may have been the case in the immediate aftermath of the election. The crucial need in this period is to develop careful and comprehensive techniques for identifying and recruiting highly qualified candidates who can fill vacancies that routinely occur in the executive branch. But the mechanisms established to do this have often failed to do so satisfactorily. The tendency remains strong throughout a president's term to focus on the seeker rather than the sought, on those who pursue appointments for themselves rather than those whom the White House ought to be pursuing. The result is a failure to exploit fully the very best talent available to the president and the country.

Recommendation 6

As soon as possible after his party's nominating convention, each major party candidate for the presidency should designate a staff to begin preparations for personnel selection and to serve as the liaison on personnel issues with the incumbent administration. Funds in the federal transition act should be allotted specifically for this purpose.

An early start on his appointment responsibilities is absolutely essential for a new president. Failure to get an early start virtually guarantees that it will take many months after the inauguration to get his administration in place and that many appointments will be hastily and haphazardly made. Both of our last two presidents have acted to get such an early start. We believe that every future president should do the same. The provision of federal transition funds especially for this purpose will eliminate the worry that personnel preparation is a diversion of resources from the campaign or that it is a signal to the electorate of overconfidence.

In our interviews with people who have participated in presidential transitions over the past several decades, we have heard repeated tales of communications breakdowns between incoming and outgoing administrations. In several cases the outgoing administration had prepared extensive briefing papers on the personnel appointment and conflict of interest clearance processes, only to have those papers disregarded by its successors. Neither the new administration nor the country is well served by this approach to the problems of transition. More extensive preelection planning for the staffing of a new administration is critical if the persistent transition problems of the past are to be avoided in the future.

Recommendation 7

To assist new administrations in identifying highly qualified candidates for presidential appointments, the national committees of the Democratic and Republican parties should each develop and maintain a permanent, up-to-date talent bank. This should be made available to the party's presidential candidate immediately after the nominating convention.

The existence of a well-maintained talent bank would greatly facilitate the immediate problem faced by every new president during the transition: identifying people with the right skills for the variety of technical and managerial jobs they have to fill. The talent bank will be especially useful if it organizes the names of candidates by the positions for which they are well qualified and if it does so for every executive position filled by presidential appointment. Because of their sensitivity to the need for appointees who share the president's philosophical inclinations and the depth of their organization throughout the country, the political party national committees are the logical place for talent banks to be maintained. We can think of few alternative repositories of this information, especially for the party out of power. A talent bank will be useful to an incoming administration only if it contains the names of candidates with genuine and abundant substantive qualifications for the jobs a president must fill. If it becomes merely a roster of political hacks, it will be of little benefit to the party or the president.

Recommendation 8

Steps should be taken immediately to prepare a set of briefing papers for new administrations that identify all of the steps formally required to effect a presidential appointment. These written materials should be gathered by the management side of the Office of Management and Budget (OMB) and made available to every major candidate for the presidency.

One of the most common difficulties encountered by newly elected presidents is that they have to construct their administrations, in the haste of a transition, with little guidance on how to go about that or on how previous administrations have done so. They do not have complete information on the nature and number of positions they have to fill, the statutory and informal requirements for each of those positions, the clearances that must be accomplished before a nomination can go forward to the Senate, or the errors and pitfalls they should be alert to avoid. This is inexcusable. Presidential transitions in the United States should not be burdened by an ignorance that could be so easily overcome.

We believe that the management side of the OMB, drawing on the experience of previous presidential personnel assistants and on the history of the appointment process provided in this and other studies, should compile a thorough set of briefing papers to be used by new administrations. At a minimum, these should include a history of the appointment process with descriptions of the patterns of organization used by previous presidents; a complete accounting of the number and character of all the positions filled by presidential appointment; a clear description of conflict of interest and other laws that affect the appointment process; samples of forms and reports that appointees must complete; and information pertaining to procedures for investigations and clearances conducted by the IRS, the FBI, and the Office of Government Ethics (OGE). In addition to preparing these briefing papers, expert career executives in the OMB should be available to serve presidential candidates as consultants on the operations of the appointment process. We believe that this will be a long step forward in reducing the confusion that usually surrounds the appointment efforts of new administrations.

Recommendation 9

As a first priority during the transition period, the president's personnel staff should establish a (fixed) timetable for interlocking political, investigatory, and conflict of interest clearances for its appointees. These should be carefully designed to minimize delay in the clearance process.

Delays in the appointment process are troublesome on two accounts. First, they impede the president's ability to lead government by retarding the emplacement of his own appointees in executive positions. Second, they leave his nominees in an unpleasant state of limbo, sometimes for as long as six months. The delays that seem to have become endemic in the past two administrations largely result from the elaborate set of clearances, especially the political ones, now employed in the appointment process.

We believe those clearances are beneficial and ought to be retained, but we do not think that they need to consume as much time as they typically have. It is the responsibility of the president, on the advice of his personnel staff, to see that (fixed) timetables are established and adhered to by all parties to the clearance process. Each government agency involved in these clearances should be provided the staff necessary to perform their responsibilities with dispatch, even if that requires the addition or reassignment of temporary staff during the transition period, when the burden of these clearances is especially large.

We believe that the clearance process can be accelerated without jeopardizing the thoroughness of investigations and without incurring prohibitive increases in cost. Genuine harm results from long delays in the appointment process, and the public interest will be well served by reducing those delays to the minimum time necessary to conduct a thorough investigation of prospective appointees.

Recommendation 10

A study of the character, coverage, and utility of the FBI's full field investigations should be conducted by the FBI, the White House personnel staff, and the Judiciary Committees of the Congress.

The full field investigation has been a routine part of the clearance process for presidential appointees since the Eisenhower administration. It is costly and time consuming. In our study we found no one who would praise the information derived from that investigation. We belive that some kind of background investigation of presidential appointees is essential. We are not persuaded, however, that the full field investigation as currently conducted serves that purpose effectively. We believe it is time for the parties most directly affected by this investigation to reexamine its conduct and utility. Our hope is that such a reexamination would produce an improved background check—one that costs less and takes less time to conduct and one that produces information more relevant to the needs of the president's personnel staff and the Senate committees responsible for confirmation.

Recommendation 11

Each president should designate, at the earliest possible date, a primary assistant for personnel. That person should be paid at Executive Level II and should have regular access to the president on personnel matters.

We make this recommendation with caution, for we believe that the organization of the White House Office should be left to each president as a matter of personal preference. We think, however, that recent history has clearly demonstrated not only that a personnel staff is now an inevitable component of the White House Office but that presidents are well served when the head of that staff is afforded the status that comes with being a senior presidential aide with direct access to the president himself. This is the best way we know for an administration to ensure the thoroughness and consistency of its appointment decisions, to minimize the influence of unwanted political pressures, and to keep the president well informed on personnel matters.

The assistant for personnel should serve as the manager of the appointment process. He or she should not make appointment decisions but should be responsible for the staff work necessary to assist the president in doing so. He or she must oversee the search and recruitment efforts of the personnel staff, ensure cordial relations with the relevant departments and agencies in the selection of nominees, and ride herd on clearance procedures to make sure they are carried out with care and dispatch.

Recommendation 12

The White House personnel staff should take a positive approach to its recruitment responsibilities. It should establish a mechanism for identifying and recruiting appointees from sources beyond those upon which presidents have traditionally relied.

For two decades presidential personnel assistants have recognized the importance of aggressive recruiting. Yet, efforts to reach out beyond those who apply for administration jobs or whose names come to the White House through political channels have only been sporadically successful. It is still the case that too much of the attention of presidential personnel staffs focuses on the seeker rather than the sought.

Until this changes, the full extent of the personnel resources available to an American president will not be adequately explored or exploited. But it will only change when presidential personnel staffs succeed in equipping themselves for the aggressive search and recruitment efforts this requires. Periodic consultation with executive search firms in the private sector should be a regular feature of this

White House function. We believe the positive approach is an important goal and that it should be a very high priority for every administration.

Recommendation 13

The president should play a visible role in the appointment process and an active part in establishing personal relationships with his own appointees.

We have been struck throughout our investigations by the frequency with which we have heard this recommendation made by former presidential personnel assistants. They are almost unanimous in identifying the importance of presidential involvement as a boost to their recruitment efforts and as a protection against exogenous political influences on appointment decisions. For a president who wants to enhance the quality of his appointments and to fortify his control over their selection, active and visible participation in the appointment process is critical.

The president can also go a long way toward increasing the enthusiasm of his appointees for the objectives of his administration by making occasional efforts to have personal contact with them. A few administrations have attempted this and have been very pleased with the results. This need not require large amounts of presidential time. Such things as making appointment announcements himself, taking part in swearing-in ceremonies, holding White House receptions for appointees, and visiting departmental headquarters can do a great deal to tighten the bonds between a president and his political executives. The long-run payoffs in mutual understanding and responsive administration more than justify the minor additions to the burden on presidential time.

Recommendation 14

The Senate should conduct an assessment of its confirmation procedures with the objective of making them more consistent across committees and of minimizing delays in the confirmation process.

The Senate plays an important constitutional role in the appointment process. We applaud the seriousness with which it has carried out that role in the past decade—a period in which Senate committees have increased their vigilance over the quality and integrity of presidential appointees. We note, however, that the confirmation process continues to be an unnecessary source of complexity and delay in the appointment process.

The principal culprits in this are the inconsistencies among committees in the information they require from nominees, in the forms they use, and in the manner in which they conduct their investigations. We recognize that different committees deal with different kinds of nominees and that some autonomy in their operations is inevitable. We believe, however, that a careful study of this would identify a number of areas in which forms could be simplified, information demands consolidated, and investigative procedures made more uniform and systematic. This would be a significant benefit to presidential personnel aides in helping nominees prepare for confirmation hearings. And, by alleviating some of the uncertainty that now permeates perceptions of the confirmation process, it would reduce the anxiety often engendered in those who must go through it.

CONFLICT OF INTEREST

Problem

Conflict of interest requirements impose two significant impediments to presidential recruiting. One is the plague of misinformation and misperception that surrounds public discussion of conflict of interest issues. The other is a number of nagging components of the conflict of interest requirements that do little to enhance the integrity of public officials and have a serious negative effect on recruitment efforts.

It is our hope that the difficulties the Reagan administration experienced in coping with the Ethics in Government Act of 1978 will have a chastening effect on future administrations and that they will better understand the requirements of the conflict of interest laws and do a better job of communicating them to potential appointees. Our finding has been that these requirements are not so burdensome as public perceptions, particularly in the business community, hold them to be. We believe that educational efforts by future presidential personnel staffs and the OGE can do a great deal to reduce the negative reaction to presidential job offers that these requirements seem to have inspired among some prospective appointees. We certainly encourage those efforts. But we also believe that there are several immediate steps that should be taken to alter the conflict of interest requirements or to facilitate their implementation.

Recommendation 15

Legislation should be enacted to ease the impact of capital gains taxes on those appointees forced to divest financial holdings in order to satisfy conflict of interest requirements.

We have found broad consensus on the importance of this recommendation. Divestiture is sometimes the only remedy for a potential conflict of interest. Often, it is costly to the appointees because of the capital gains taxes they must pay on the appreciated value of their assets and because it is usually not possible to spread that tax liability over several years. While we support divestiture as a necessary cure for conflicts of interest in some cases, we do not believe that appointees should have to endure heavy financial penalties as a cost of entering government service. That is a matter of fairness; it is also a critical recruiting issue. We believe that this recommendation is a positive step in both regards.

Recommendation 16

Congress should amend the Ethics in Government Act to clarify and simplify the blind trust provisions.

Again, we recognize the utility of blind trusts in preventing potential conflicts of interest. We believe, however, that the blind trust laws are unnecessarily confusing and restrictive.

The OGE has made three recommendations for amendments to the blind trust provisions of the Ethics in Government Act. We support all three. The first would allow all executive branch officials, not just those subject to Senate confirmation, to have the option of establishing qualified, diversified blind trusts. The second would allow parties to an "old family trust"—a trust established by an ancestor for the benefit of a person who becomes a government official—to agree to make the trust blind to the government official who is a beneficiary. The third calls on the Congress to clarify the category of "excepted trusts" by defining what constitutes "no knowledge."

These are straightforward and good ideas, and we believe that each would improve the usefulness of blind trusts as remedies for potential conflicts of interest.

Recommendation 17

Financial reporting requirements should be made consistent across the government. Wherever possible within the spirit of the conflict of interest laws, the number of reporting categories should be reduced.

Our inquiries have produced a number of complaints about the extraordinary complexity of financial disclosure forms. It is now routine for any prospective appointee with even a moderate degree of personal wealth to feel compelled to employ an accountant or an attorney or both for assistance in completing these forms, thus adding to the cost of entering government service.

We hope that the appropriate officials will make continuing efforts to simplify these reporting requirements. One important way in which this could occur would be for ethics officials in the executive branch and in Congress to negotiate agreement on standardization of the reporting forms that they use. This would be a substantial improvement on the current situation in which appointees are required to fill out a bewildering array of different forms, all asking for the same information sliced different ways.

We also believe it possible to achieve a simplification in the current requirement that financial holdings be reported in six categories of magnitude. We recognize the need for a broad lower category that identifies the existence of a potential conflict and for an upper level benchmark to indicate a holding of such value as to suggest the possibility of an extensive financial relationship. We have been able to find little purpose for categories in between, however. Our conversations with officials who review these statements indicate that they find little value in them. We believe that no interest would be harmed by reducing the number of reporting categories.

Recommendation 18

Waivers of conflict of interest laws should be more frequently granted by agency ethics officials in cases where the small size of a financial holding or the insignificance of a financial relationship makes the possibility of conflict of interest very remote. The OGE should publish guidelines for agency officials to use in granting these waivers.

There is a statutory basis for the granting of waivers; this is not an improper circumvention of the conflict of interest laws. The waiver provision was included in the statutes to permit common sense to prevail in the case of holdings or relationships that posed no significant threat of becoming a conflict of interest. Experience indicates, however, that agency officials have been reluctant to grant waivers because they have few available precedents to guide them and because they worry about the political repercussions of appearing too casual about implementing conflict of interest laws.

We believe that agency ethics officials would be less reluctant to grant waivers in cases where those were justified if they had written guidance from the OGE on how and when to do this. We believe that these guidelines would serve as the basis for a governmentwide policy on the granting of waivers and would reduce the burden of decision that currently seems to fall on each agency head and ethics counsellor individually. We further believe that this would lead, in the long run, to more frequent use of this useful provision of the conflict of interest laws and that this would ease the problems of compliance for presidential appointees.

EASING THE TRANSITION OF NEW APPOINTEES INTO GOVERNMENT SERVICE

Problem

During the course of this study, we have had discussions with a number of present and former presidential appointees. One of the concerns that emerged most prominently from those discussions is the failure of the government to provide adequate assistance to new appointees in making the transition from the private to the public sector.

This is a difficult period for someone coming into government for the first time. There is the logistical problem of moving to Washington. Private sector employment has to be terminated. The appointee's personal financial affairs must be put in order. There are doubts, often very large doubts, about adapting to public life. There is a new job to master. And there is a confirmation hearing for which to prepare.

In all of these matters, new appointees would benefit substantially from the help of experienced hands. But that help is available only to some and only sporadically. The executive branch has never paid adequate attention to the transitional needs of its new appointees. Its failure to do so has made the entry into public life more worrisome than it needs to be and, in some cases, has prevented people from accepting offers of presidential appointments.

Recommendation 19

The federal government should reimburse presidential appointees for all reasonable moving costs incurred when they enter the government.

We doubt seriously that anyone disagrees with the appropriateness of this proposal. The federal government pays moving costs for its career executives and its military personnel when they move from one assignment to another. We see no reason its noncareer executives should be treated differently. Many presidential appointees accept a significant cut in salary when they move from the private to the public sector. We think it is counterproductive for the government to impose a further financial sacrifice on those people by requiring them to absorb their own moving expenses as well.

The number of new appointees moving to Washington in any given year is not very large. Reimbursement of their moving expenses would place no great burden on the federal treasury, but it would remove a great burden from presidential appointees. And it would eliminate this nagging and unnecessary impediment to presidential recruiting.

Recommendation 20

The White House personnel office, the Federal Executive Institute, and qualified nongovernmental organizations should work together to develop comprehensive orientation programs for noncareer executives. These should be offered whenever there is a change in administrations and at least twice a year thereafter.

We believe that all noncareer executives can benefit from participation in a program that introduces them to the political environment in which they will be operating; that advises them on how to survive and prosper in that environment; and that provides them basic information on such things as the media, the annual budget cycle, the nature of decisionmaking in Congress, the structure of the White House, and the character of the career service. We also believe that people coming from business corporations would find it an advantage to hear from others who had preceded them and had successfully made the transition from the private to the public sector.

Occasional past efforts to provide this kind of orientation program have been given very positive evaluations by those who participated. Among the best of those was the orientation program implemented in the Ford administration. Its utility underlines not only the benefits that derive from such programs but also the importance of having the president participate in them directly. There is no more effective way to attract the interest and ensure the attendance of busy new executives than to hold orientation programs in the White House with the president involved. We commend the Ford administration's approach to this, and we regret that so few other administrations have emulated it. We believe that orientation programs for new appointees should become a normal component of the appointment process and that they should be offered regularly enough so that every new presidential appointee has the opportunity to participate in them.

Recommendation 21

A specific group within the White House personnel staff should be assigned responsibility for providing support and assistance to nominees from the time of their selection until they are confirmed by the Senate.

In recent administrations, the White House personnel staff has lacked the time and the inclination to help its nominees navigate the appointment and confirmation processes. Once they accept the president's offer of an appointment, they are typically left to fend for themselves in the trying and confusing period before the nomination is confirmed. We believe that this is not the kind of decent treatment a first-class employer should provide its new employees and, more importantly, that it lengthens the time it takes for appointees to get up to speed in their new positions.

One of the things the personnel office could do during this period is to provide nominees with written or oral descriptions of the jobs for which they have been selected. Odd as it may seem, many nominees are left in the dark about this, not knowing exactly what their responsibilities will be or why they were selected to fill a particular position at a particular time. We see no reason to perpetuate this obvious flaw in the appointment process, especially when written job descriptions are often readily available.

Another easily remedied source of confusion in the appointment process is the manner in which nominees are guided through the task of filling out and submitting the bewildering array of personal information and conflict of interest forms that are now mandatory. Typically, nominees are given a mass (and a mess) of paperwork, in different sizes and formats, often without adequate instructions, and are then rarely provided with any significant assistance from the personnel office in completing this paperwork. We believe that a simple first step to improving the ease with which new appointees move into their jobs would be for the White House to design and provide for each nominee a packet of materials including all the necessary forms with clear instructions, written advice on dealing with common conflict of interest concerns, suggestions for preparing for confirmation hearings, and so on. Changes in this direction are long overdue.

We believe that it would be a great improvement on current practice for a subunit of the White House personnel office to serve as "preparation advisers" for new appointees. These advisers could provide assistance to nominees in moving to Washington, completing conflict of interest reviews and other clearances, making acquaintances and receiving substantive briefings from their new departments, and preparing for confirmation hearings. Whatever other benefits this would produce—and we believe it would produce many—it would certainly help reduce the anxieties and uncertainties that are common accompaniments to the move from a job in the private sector to an executive position in the federal government.

COMPENSATION

Problem

As we indicated earlier, our principal concern has not been with the general issue of government compensation but rather with its impact on the recruitment of noncareer executives. Our finding is that salary levels are not a serious impediment in recruiting cabinet officers or other senior-level officials but that they are an impediment in recruiting excellent people from the private sector to fill midlevel executive and technical positions in the subcabinet. The prestige and "psychic income" afforded by these positions is often not sufficient to compensate for the relatively low salaries they provide. The result is that salary sometimes becomes a large negative factor in the recruiting calculus.

Recommendation 22

The Congress should act to end the linkage of congressional and Executive Level II salaries. Congressional and executive salaries should be determined separately.

Calls for breaking the link between congressional and executive salaries began almost as soon as that practice was initiated. The last quadrennial commission clearly reiterated that call. We recognize the difficulty Congress faces—or that any legislative body faces—in voting to raise its own salaries. We do not expect that to change at any time soon. But we regret that executive salaries have to be held hostage to the timidity of legislators about raising their own salaries.

We would also note that linkage has not created the intended equivalence between legislative and Executive Level II salaries. Members of Congress have access to perquisites and fringe benefits—most notably, to the legal right to earn outside income—that are denied to executive branch employees. When the value of these is considered, there is often a substantial gap between legislative and executive compensation.

We believe that linkage is the principal reason that midlevel executive salaries have been allowed to lose much of their purchasing power and to fall further behind private sector salaries in the last decade. We know that presidential recruiting has been harmed by that. We believe the public interest will be well served when an end is put to the practice of linking executive and congressional salaries.

CONCLUSION

We have included here no recommendations for sweeping reforms of the presidential appointment process. We believe that the existing White House structure for personnel selection and the procedures developed within it provide an appropriate framework for the sensible management of the appointment process. Within that framework, however, we have identified a number of areas in which we think improvements can be made. We believe that, if successfully implemented, the cumulative impact of all of our recommendations will be a substantial improvement in the operations of the appointment process and in the quality of the people it brings into government service.

Appointment choices are critically important to the effectiveness of the federal government. Taken together, they are probably as important in their consequences as are the electoral choices that Americans make at the polls. We hope that our analyses and recommendations will bring a higher level of excellence to the appointment process. We also hope that this study will focus attention on this important process and thereby encourage broad discussion of how it should be organized and operated. We are convinced that the success of the appointment process is as dependent on popular interest and concern as is the success of the electoral process in serving the needs of the American people. If this book helps to stimulate that interest and concern, we will have accomplished a good deal of what we set out to do.

BIBLIOGRAPHY

Adams, Bruce. "The Limitations of Muddling Through: Does Anyone in Washington Really Think Anymore?" *Public Administration Review* 39 (November/December 1979): 545-52.

Adams, Bruce, and Kathryn Kavanagh-Baran. *Promise and Performance: Carter Builds a New Administration.* Lexington, Mass.: Lexington Books, 1979.

Graham, James M., and Victor H. Kramer. *Appointments To The Regulatory Agencies: The Federal Communications Commission And The Federal Trade Commission, 1949-1974* (Printed for the use of the Senate Committee on Commerce.) Washington, D.C.: U.S. Government Printing Office, 1976.

Hartman, Robert W., and Arnold R. Weber, eds. *The Rewards of Public Service*, Washington, D.C.: Brookings Institution, 1980.

Heclo, Hugh, *A Government of Strangers*, Washington, D.C.: Brookings Institution, 1977.

Mackenzie, G. Calvin. "The Paradox of Presidential Personnel Management." Chapter 4 in Hugh Heclo and Lester M. Salamon, eds., *The Illusion of Presidential Government.* Boulder: Westview Press, 1981.

____ . *The Politics of Presidential Appointments.* New York: Free Press, 1981.

Macy, John W., Jr. *Public Service.* New York: Harper & Row, 1971.

Malek, Frederic V. *Washington's Hidden Tragedy: The Failure to Make Government Work.* New York: Free Press, 1978.

Mann, Dean E., and Jameson W. Doig. *The Assistant Secretaries: Problems and Processes of Appointment.* Washington, D.C.: Brookings Institution, 1965.

Nathan, Richard. *The Administrative Presidency.* New York: Wiley, 1983.

Perkins, Roswell. "The New Federal Conflict of Interest Law." *Harvard Law Review* 76 (April 1963): 1113.

U.S. Commission on Executive, Legislative and Judicial Salaries. *Report of the Commission on Executive, Legislative and Judicial Salaries.* Washington, D.C.: U.S. Government Printing Office, 1976.

U.S. Commission on Executive, Legislative and Judicial Salaries. *Report of the Commission on Executive, Legislative and Judicial Salaries.* Washington, D.C.: U.S. Government Printing Office, 1980.

Stanley, David T. *Changing Administrations: The 1961 and 1964 Transitions in Six Departments.* Washington, D.C.: Brookings Institution, 1965.

____ . *Men Who Govern: A Biographical Profile of Federal Political Executives.* Washington, D.C.: Brookings Institution, 1967.

U.S. House of Representatives, 94th Congress, 2d Session, (1976), Committee on Post Office and Civil Service, Subcommittee on Manpower and Civil Service. *Final Report on Violations and Abuses of Merit Principles in Federal Employment* (Committee print). Washington, D.C.: U.S. Government Printing Office, 1976.

U.S. Senate, 95th Congress, 1st Session (1977), Committee on Government Operations. *Study on Federal Regulation, Volume I: The Regulatory Appointments Process* (Committee print). Washington, D.C.: U.S. Government Printing Office, 1977.

Walter, J. Jackson. "The Ethics in Government Act, Conflict of Interest Laws and Presidential Recruiting," *Public Administration Review* 41 (November/December 1981): 659-65.

INDEX

ABOUT THE AUTHORS

John W. Macy, Jr., a graduate of Wesleyan University, has had a diversified management and consulting career in government, business, academia, and nonprofit organizations. His service as executive director (1953–58) and chairman (1961–69) of the Civil Service Commission involved him in personnel policymaking and administration of the federal workforce. In addition, he served as personnel assistant to President Lyndon Johnson. In other executive assignments, Macy was the first president of the Corporation for Public Broadcasting, president of the Council of Better Business Bureaus, and president of Development and Resources Corporation. He served as the first director of the Federal Emergency Management Agency from 1979 to 1981. Mr. Macy is a former president of the American Society of Public Administration and has been a member of the National Academy of Public Administration since 1969.

J. Jackson Walter has been president of the National Academy of Public Administration since September 1982. A graduate of Amherst College and Yale Law School, he practiced law in Boston until becoming secretary of the Department of Business Regulation for the State of Florida. In 1979 he was appointed by President Jimmy Carter to be the first director of the Office of Government Ethics. He was reappointed to that position by President Ronald Reagan in 1981.

Bruce Adams has written a number of articles on public administration and governance and is co-author of *Promise and Performance: Carter Builds a New Administration* (Lexington Books, 1979), a study of President Carter's initial personnel appointments. Mr. Adams, a Charles F. Kettering Foundation Fellow, has served as a fellow of the Institute of Politics at the John F. Kennedy School of Government at Harvard University and as director of issue development for Common Cause. A graduate of Princeton University and the Georgetown University Law Center, Mr. Adams is a former chairman of the Montgomery County (Maryland) Charter Review Commission and a member of the Maryland Governor's Salary Commission.

G. Calvin Mackenzie served as senior consultant for this project. He is a graduate of Bowdoin College and holds a Ph.D. in Government from Harvard University. Mr. Mackenzie has written widely on the presidency and the problems of personnel management in the federal executive branch. He is the author of *The Politics of Presidential Appointments* (Free Press, 1981) and co-editor of *The House at Work* (University of Texas Press, 1981), a study of the administration of the U.S. House of Representatives. Mr. Mackenzie has served as a consultant to several congressional committees and was senior research analyst for the U.S. House Commission on Administrative Review. He is currently associate professor of government and director of the Public Policy Program at Colby College in Waterville, Maine.